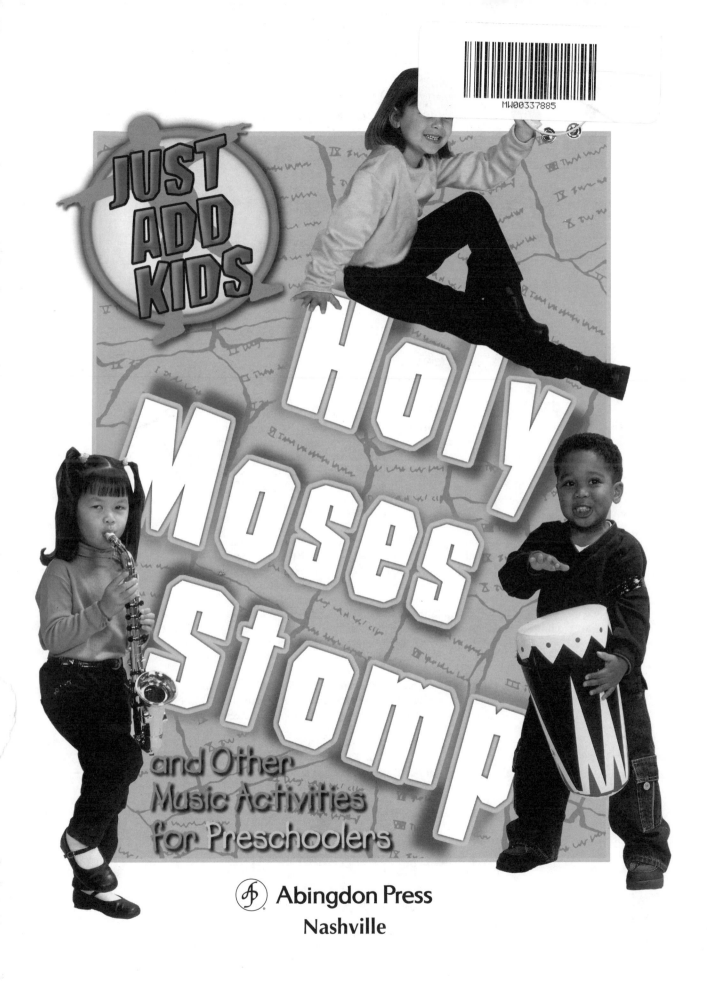

JUST ADD KIDS

Holy Moses Stomp

and Other Music Activities for Preschoolers

Abingdon Press
Nashville

Just Add Kids: Holy Moses Stomp and other Bible Music Activities for Preschoolers

ISBN 0-687-03069-2

Lead Editor: Daphna Flegal
Editor: Linda Ray Miller
Production Editors: Theresa P. Kuhr and Betsi H. Smith
Designers: Paige Easter and Mark Foltz
Illustrations (sign language) by: Robert S. Jones
© 1997, 1998, 1999, 2000 Abingdon Press
Additional illustrations by:
Barbara Upchurch, p. 21 – © 1996 Cokesbury
Megan Jeffery, pp. 44, 103 – © 2002 Abingdon Press
Jack Kershner, pp. 68–71 – © 2001 Cokesbury
Nell Fisher, p. 72 – © 2000 Cokesbury
Cover and Inside Photographs: Ron Benedict, UMPH Photography Staff

00 01 02 03 04 05 06 07 08 09—10 9 8 7 6 5 4 3 2 1

MANUFACTURED IN THE UNITED STATES OF AMERICA

Preschool Music Activities
Table of Contents

Introduction
Welcome to Just Add Kids

Get ready for a great experience in music. HOLY MOSES STOMP AND OTHER MUSIC ACTIVITIES FOR PRESCHOOLERS is loaded with songs, games, movement, and activities that are interactive, meaningful, and fun. HOLY MOSES STOMP uses music as a springboard to get children involved in the Bible story. One day they're acting out the story as they listen to it being sung. Another day they're listening to instrumental music and moving to show how Bible people must have felt. Or they could be just plain having fun with the music while hearing how much God loves them. Best of all, you, the teacher, don't have to have ANY musical training at all to use this resource. The only thing you have to know is how to run a CD player!

Each child in your class is unique, with his or her own family background and experiences. But preschoolers do have some common traits. Understanding those traits will help you in your classroom:

- Preschoolers have lots of energy. They enjoy movement, although they are still struggling with fine motor skills.
- Preschoolers love anything silly, whether they're laughing, saying nonsense words, or singing a fun song. They are learning to identify colors and shapes.
- Preschoolers are just beginning to share. They are learning to interact, to respect others' feelings, and to wait until it's their turn. They may have a hard time leaving their parents.

For guidelines on how to make the most out of your music time, see the article on the next page. For other resources that will help you make your class time the best that it can be, don't miss the other books in the *Just Add Kids* collection:

- *Footprints on the Wall and 50 Other Bible Crafts for Preschoolers*
- *Ring 'Round Jericho and 50 Other Bible Games for Preschoolers*
- *Don't Get Wet Feet and 50 Other Bible Stories for Preschoolers*

And if you want to use music with older children, check out:

- *Rockin' Rainsticks and Other Bible Music Activities for Elementary Children*

Preschool Music

Using Music to Teach God's Word

Children learn as they respond to and enjoy music. As they sing "Away in a Manger," they learn details about the Nativity and add words such as *manger* to their vocabulary. As they dance with scarf to "Creation Music," they learn about the many facets of God's creation. And what deeper theological truth can you teach children than, "Jesus loves me this I know, for the Bible tells me so"?

Using music also helps to focus a class. Many times I have quieted a rowdy class simply by starting to sing a song. When I have their attention, I can sing softer and slower until the entire class is settled and ready for the next activity.

One of the best ways to include music is to use it to signal transitions. Singing "A Helper I Will Be" is a gentle reminder that play time is over. Hearing "Praise God" can be a signal that it is time to come to the circle.

Follow these simple guidelines to use music successfully in your classroom:

- **Be safe.** If the activity involves movement, clear the area of hazards. Remove any rugs that can move or trip a child. Move furniture out of the way. Make sure there are no sharp edges on tables or countertops.

- **Be prepared.** Do not gather the children and THEN try to locate the CD or the instruments. Have everything ready once you have the children's attention.

- **Be aware of disabilities**. If a child has hearing problems, use big motions to convey the tempo and the beat of the music. If the child has a mobility problem, adapt any activity that involves movement.

- **Keep it age-level appropriate.** Preschoolers cannot remember the words to long songs. Nor can they sing songs with very high or very low pitches. Some songs are more for dancing than singing.

- **Have fun.** Music is meant to be active, and it will be up to you to lead the children in the motions and responses. Don't be shy. Enjoy yourself, and enjoy watching the children have fun. The motions and responses will help the children remember what you are teaching them, and isn't that what's important?

OLD TESTAMENT

The Bible: The Book of God's Word

by Lora Jean Gowan

Here Is the Bible

Supplies: "The B-I-B-L-E" (page 9), CD, CD player, Bibles

Sing the song "The B-I-B-L-E" (page 9) with the children. Choose a Bible that has the word *Bible* printed in large letters on the front cover. Point to each letter as indicated in the song.

If you have enough Bibles, have each child hold a Bible in her or his lap. Sing the song again and encourage the children to point to the letters on their Bibles.

Say: Let's pretend our hands are Bibles.

Lead the children in the suggested motions as you say the following poem:

Open it; (*Hold hands together as an open book.*)
Shut it; (*Place palms together.*)
Open it; (*Open hands.*)
Shut it; (*Place palms together.*)
Read it every day. (*Point to eyes.*)

Open it; (*Open hands.*)
Shut it; (*Place palms together.*)
Open it; (*Open hands.*)
Shut it; (*Place palms together.*)
It will show God's way. (*Cross hands over heart.*)

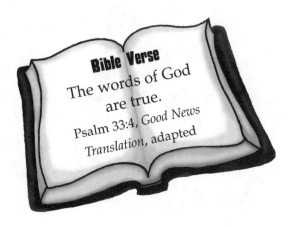

Bible Verse
The words of God are true.
Psalm 33:4, *Good News Translation*, adapted

8

The B-I-B-L-E

The B - I - B - L - E! Yes,

that's the book for me! I stand a - lone on the

Word of God. The B - I - B - L - E!

WORDS: Traditional
MUSIC: Traditional; arr. John D. Horman
Arr. © 2000 Cokesbury

Songs marked with this symbol are recorded on the CD. The number # indicates the appropriate track.

Creation

It Is Very Good

Help the children celebrate the senses that God gave them by teaching them the following litany. First teach the refrain: "It is good. It is good. It is very good." Then encourage them to name the things that God made.

Bright blue skies and fluffy clouds,
Soft green grass and pink seashells,
I like what I see in God's world.
What do you like to see? (*Repeat things the children name.*)
It is good. It is good. It is very good!

Singing birds and chirping bugs,
Quacking ducks and laughing friends,
I like what I hear in God's world.
What do you like to hear? (*Repeat things the children name.*)
It is good. It is good. It is very good!

Purple grapes and yellow squash,
Apple juice and small green peas,
I like what I taste in God's world.
What do you like to taste? (*Repeat things the children name.*)
It is good. It is good. It is very good!

Cold snowflakes and kittens' fur,
Squishy mud and Grandma's hug,
I like what I touch in God's world.
What do you like to touch? (*Repeat things the children name.*)
It is good. It is good. It is very good!

Popping corn and one red rose,
Tall pine trees and fresh damp earth,
I like what I smell in God's world.
What do you like to smell? (*Repeat things the children name.*)
It is good. It is good. It is very good!

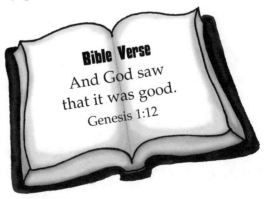

Bible Verse
And God saw
that it was good.
Genesis 1:12

Praise God's Creation

Supplies: Bible

In your own words, tell the story of Creation found in Genesis 1:1–2:4. Point out what God created on each day.

Develop simple movements or sounds that correspond with a line of the act of praise printed below (for example, make gurgling sounds for water.)

Lead the act of praise. The children will respond with the appropriate movement or sound at the end of each phrase. Then, everyone will respond by enthusiastically saying: "Praise God! Tell about the wonderful things God has done!"

In the beginning, God created the heavens and the earth,
God created day and night. (*sound*)
Praise God! Tell about the wonderful things God has done!

God created sky, earth, and water. (*sound*)
Praise God! Tell about the wonderful things God has done!

God created so many plants. (*sound*)
Praise God! Tell about the wonderful things God has done!

God created the fish and sea animals. (*sound*)
Praise God! Tell about the wonderful things God has done!

God created the birds and flying creatures. (*sound*)
Praise God! Tell about the wonderful things God has done!

God created large and small animals, pets, and wild animals. (*sound*)
Praise God! Tell about the wonderful things God has done!

God created all kinds of people. (*sound*)
Praise God! Tell about the wonderful things God has done!

God's creation is very good. (*sound*)
Praise God! Tell about the wonderful things God has done!

Sing About Creation

Supplies: "The Creation" (page 13)

Sing "The Creation" (page 13) to the tune of "This Is the Way." Have the children sign the word *good* whenever it is sung in the song. (Sign language is also on page 13.)

Stretch and Praise

Supplies: "God Plans for Every Growing Thing" (below), CD, CD player

Squat down and touch the ground as you sing the first phrase of the song "God Plans for Every Growing Thing" (below). Slowly stand up and reach for the sky as you sing the second phrase.

God Plans for Every Growing Thing

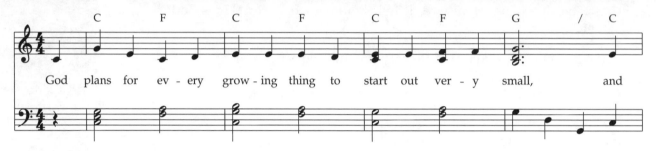

God plans for ev-ery grow-ing thing to start out ver-y small, and

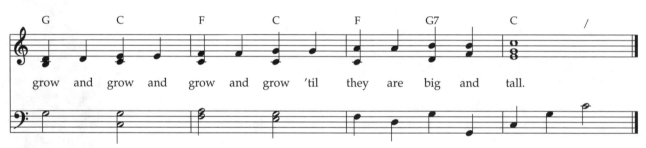

grow and grow and grow and grow 'til they are big and tall.

WORDS: Jo Risser
MUSIC: Jane Blessoe; arr. by Carol M. Frazier

© 1993 Cokesbury

CD Track #2

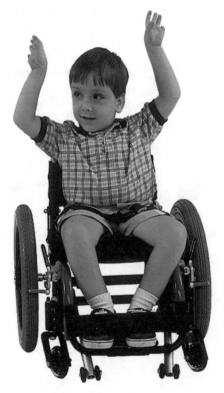

12

The Creation

| F | / | F | / | C7 | / | C7 | / |

1. God made the sun and moon and stars, moon and stars, moon and stars.
(Hold arms in circle over head for sun and moon. Hold arms over head and wiggle fingers for stars.)

| F | / | F | / | C7 | / | F | / |

God made the sun and moon and stars, and saw that it was good.
(Make sign for good. Touch fingers of right hand to lips. Move hand forward. Drop it to the open palm of the left hand.)

2. God made the earth and sky and seas, sky and seas, sky and seas.
   (Touch the floor for earth. Reach arms up for sky. Wave arms in front of you for seas.)
   God made the earth and sky and seas, and saw that it was good.
   (Repeat sign for good.)

3. God made the seeds and plants and trees, plants and trees, plants and trees.
   (Crouch down and slowly stand with arms above head.)
   God made the seeds and plants and trees, and saw that it was good.
   (Repeat sign for good.)

4. God made the fish and birds and bees, birds and bees, birds and bees.
   (Put palms together and wiggle hands for fish. Flap arms for birds and bees.)
   God made the fish and birds and bees, and saw that it was good.
   (Repeat sign for good.)

5. God made the cows and creeping things, creeping things, creeping things.
   (Take small, creeping steps.)
   God made the cows and creeping things, and saw that it was good.
   (Repeat sign for good.)

6. God made people like you and me, you and me, you and me.
   (Point to others. Point to self.)
   God made people like you and me, and saw that it was good.
   (Repeat sign for good.)

7. God rested on the seventh day, seventh day, seventh day.
   (Hold hands under head as if sleeping.)
   God rested on the seventh day, for it was very good.
   (Repeat sign for good.)

WORDS: Daphna Flegal (based on Genesis 1:1–2:3)
MUSIC: Traditional
Words © 1997 Abingdon Press

Swim Like a Fish

Supplies: "God Planned for Fish" (below)

Sing to the tune of "Mary Had a Little Lamb."

As the children sing "God Planned for Fish" (below), have them place their palms together and move hands back and forth like a fish swimming. Then let them add the following verses and motions.

God planned for crabs to walk this way,
  walk this way, walk this way.
God planned for crabs to walk this way
  in the deep blue sea. (*Walk sideways.*)

God planned for dogs to bark this way,
  bark this way, bark this way.
God planned for dogs to bark this way
  by the deep blue sea. (*Make barking sounds.*)

God planned for flowers to grow this way,
  grow this way, grow this way.
God planned for flowers to grow this way
  by the deep blue sea. (*Crouch down low, then stand up.*)

God planned for water to move this way,
  move this way, move this way.
God planned for water to move this way
  in the deep blue sea. (*Wave hands up and down.*)

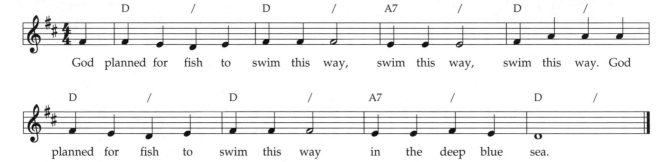

WORDS: Sts. 1-2, Daphna Flegal; sts. 3, 4, 5 Linda Ray Miller
MUSIC: Traditional

Words sts. 1-2 © 1996 Cokesbury; sts. 3, 4, 5 © 2001 Abingdon Press, admin. by The Copyright Co., Nashville, TN

Sing to the tune of "Mary Had a Little Lamb"

God Planned for Light

by Joyce Riffe and Linda Ray Miller

Encourage the children to do the motions as you say the poem below.

God planned for light so I can see. (*Point to eyes.*)
God planned for light to help warm me. (*Hug arms.*)
God planned for light to make the day. (*Spread arms.*)
I am so glad God planned that way. (*Place hand at chest as you say, "I."*)

God planned for sky and wind to blow. (*Wave arms as in the wind.*)
God planned for water down below. (*Wave hands as if making waves.*)
God planned for dirt so I can play. (*Run in place.*)
I am so glad God planned that way. (*Place hand at chest as you say, "I."*)

God planned for trees to grow so tall. (*Stretch up high.*)
God planned for flowers very small. (*Touch the ground.*)
God planned for food for every day. (*Rub stomach.*)
I am so glad God planned that way. (*Place hand at chest as you say, "I."*)

God planned for birds up in the sky. (*Flap arms.*)
God planned for goats to climb so high. (*Pretend to climb.*)
God planned for fish down in the bay. (*Place palms together; wiggle hands.*)
I am so glad God planned that way. (*Place hand at chest as you say, "I."*)

God planned for eyes so I can see. (*Point to eyes.*)
God planned for hair to cover me. (*Put hands on head.*)
God planned for hands to help me pray. (*Fold hands as in prayer.*)
I am so glad God planned that way. (*Place hand at chest as you say, "I."*)

Creation Dance

by Sandi McGarrah

Supplies: "Creation Dance" (CD), CD player, scarfs or streamers

Have the children close their eyes and listen to the music of "Creation Dance" (CD). Give each child a scarf or a streamer. Ask them to imagine their color represents a part of creation (for example, blue for water, green for trees, yellow for sun, red for birds or flowers).

Ask the children to move to the music of creation in the way they think their color would move.

After a period of time have the children trade colors as the music continues.

As you listen again to "Creation Dance," lead the children in the suggested motions as you read the following. You may wish to practice saying the lines with the music before actually leading the children.

In the beginning, there was nothing. The universe was empty and had no shape. (*Have children get close to the ground and cover their heads.*) Then God said, "Let there be light!" And the light appeared! God saw that it was good. (*Have children uncover their heads and stand to move to the music.*) "But wait," said God. "What shall I do with the darkness? It is good too!" So God separated the light and the dark and called the dark, night. (*Have the children close their eyes.*) Then in the night, God placed twinkling stars, shooting stars, and the big round moon! And God saw that it was good! (*Have the children pretend to be twinkling stars, shooting stars, and big round moons.*) Evening passed and the morning came. That was the end of the day. God was very pleased with the creation. God saw that it was good!

CD Track #3

Creation Transitions

Use movement to help your children transition from activity to activity. For example, when it is time to move from learning centers to story time, ask the children to come to the story circle in one of the following ways:

1. **Say:** Let's each pretend to be the sun. It is day. Make your sun shine all around the room. (*Encourage the children to hold their arms outward or upward in circles and move around the room.*) Everyone stop. (*Whisper.*) Now let's each pretend to be the moon. It is night. Make the moon shine all the way to the story area. When you reach the story area, please find a seat. (*Encourage the children to hold their arms outward or upward in circles, move to the story area, and then sit down.*)

2. **Say:** God made the water and saw that it was good. Let's pretend to swim in the great new waters! Stand where you are and swim to me! (You may change the type of strokes the children use: back stroke, butterfly, or freestyle!)

3. **Say:** In the Bible we learn that God created all kinds of beautiful plants. Please stand where you are and pretend I am the sun. My rays are warm and loving. Now pretend you are a tiny plant. Move toward me slowly with your arms stretched high! Grow little plants! Move toward the sun until you reach the story area. Now find a seat!

4. Call the children by name, either one at a time or in groups of two or three. Direct the children to move to your story area with the following suggestions.

   Pretend you are a turtle and move slo-o-o-wly to our story time.
   Pretend you are a kangaroo and hop, hop, to our story time.
   Pretend you are a bird and fly across the sky to our story time.
   Pretend you are a s-s-s-snake and s-s-s-slither to our story time.
   Pretend you are a fish and swim to our story time.
   Pretend you are a horse and gallop to our story time.
   Pretend you are an elephant, swing your trunk to our story time.

Continue the game until all the children are seated.

Noah

Act Like Animals

CD Track #4

Supplies: "Noah" (below), CD, CD player

Talk to the children about the different ways that animals move and sound.
Sing "Noah," making the motions below as you sing each verse:

Verse 1: Hold both hands up beside your face with palms forward and fingers
bent as if you had claws.
Verse 2: Hold one hand with the index and middle finger extended (making a "V").
Make your hand "hop" across in front of you.
Verse 3: Place your hands in your armpits and "flap" your elbows as if they were wings.
Verse 4: Wave your arms over your head as if swinging from trees.
Verse 5: Squat down and bounce without moving your feet.
Verse 6: Clasp your hands in front of you and swing them like an elephant's trunk.
Stomp your feet.
Verse 7: Place one hand under your chin, like a beard, and wiggle your fingers.
Verse 8: Stretch your arms out and fly like a bird (without moving.)

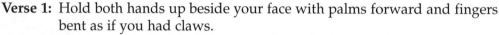

WORDS and MUSIC: Marsha Marshall
© 1979 Marsha Marshall. Used by permission.

Color a Rainbow

Supplies: "Rainbow Song" (below), large piece of paper, marker, colored tissue paper, glue

Place a large piece of paper on the wall. Draw arcs on the paper to form the outline of a rainbow. Ask the children to glue scraps of colored tissue paper within the outlines. Encourage them to fill each arc with the same color, but don't worry too much if the pieces are scattered across the rainbow pattern.

Tell the children that all rainbows are different and that God likes variety. Sing the song "Rainbow Song" (below) while admiring your paper rainbow. (This song is sung to the tune of "This Old Man.")

Bible Verse
I am putting my rainbow in the clouds.
Genesis 9:13, Good News Translation, adapted

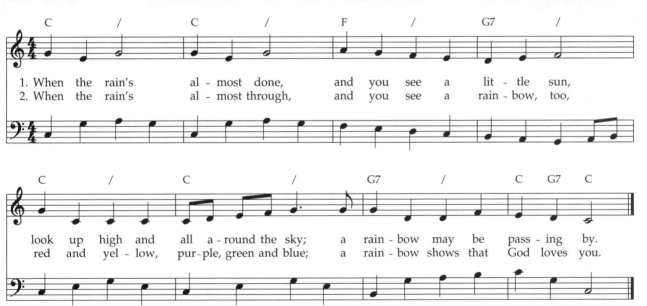

1. When the rain's al-most done, and you see a lit-tle sun,
2. When the rain's al-most through, and you see a rain-bow, too,

look up high and all a-round the sky; a rain-bow may be pass-ing by.
red and yel-low, pur-ple, green and blue; a rain-bow shows that God loves you.

WORDS: Pat Floyd
MUSIC: Traditional

Words © 1987 Graded Press, admin. by The Copyright Co., Nashville, TN

Sing to the tune of "This Old Man"

Noah's Choir

Supplies: "The Animals on the Ark" (page 21), posterboard, scissors, stapler and staples, glue, construction paper, yarn

Sing "The Animals on the Ark" to the tune of "The Wheels on the Bus."

Before class: Cut posterboard into strips about six inches wide and thirty inches long.

Ask the children to list animals that make a sound. Let the children become those animals by making forehead masks based on masks from the Northwest Coast Native American tradition.

Staple a posterboard strip around each child's head. This should leave a long portion of the strip out in front of the forehead to make an animal's head. Glue the strips left in front together. Cut the shape of an animal head in the strip.

Encourage the children to use scraps of posterboard, construction paper, and yarn to make animal heads from the head strips.

Have the children wear their masks and form a circle and sit down. Sing "The Animals on the Ark," adding verses to include each mask that the children have made. Let each child stand as his or her verse is sung.

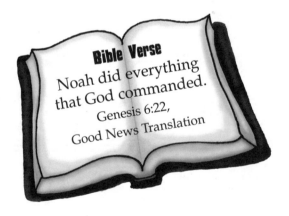

Bible Verse
Noah did everything that God commanded.
Genesis 6:22,
Good News Translation

The Animals on the Ark

1. The cows _ on the ark go moo, moo, moo, moo, moo, moo, moo, moo, moo.
2. The bun-nies on the ark go hop, hop, hop, hop, hop, hop, hop, hop, hop.
3. The ducks _ on the ark go quack, quack, quack, quack, quack, quack, quack, quack, quack.
4. The bees _ on the ark go buzz, buzz, buzz, buzz, buzz, buzz, buzz, buzz, buzz.

The cows _ on the ark go moo, moo, moo, walk - ing side by side.
The bun-nies on the ark go hop, hop, hop, hop - ping side by side.
The ducks _ on the ark go quack, quack, quack, wad - dling side by side.
The bees _ on the ark go buzz, buzz, buzz, fly - ing side by side.

WORDS: Daphna Flegal (based on Genesis 6:19-22)
MUSIC: Traditional
Words © 1997 Abingdon Press, admin. by The Copyright Co., Nashville, TN

Sing to the tune of "The Wheels on the Bus"

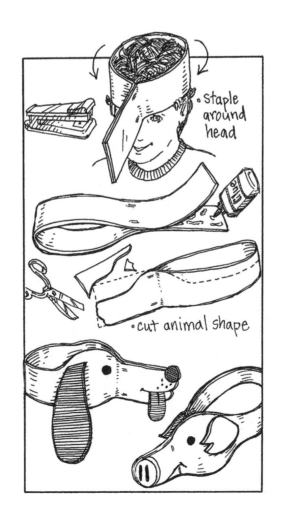

staple around head

cut animal shape

Abraham and Sarah

God Blessed Abraham

Supplies: "Abraham's Blessing" (below)

Tell the story of Abraham and Sarah.

Say: No matter where Abraham and Sarah went, God stayed with them and blessed them. Abraham and Sarah were children of God. (*Then tell the story of Isaac and Rebekah.*) God loved and blessed Isaac and Rebekah too. Isaac and Rebekah were children of God.

Sing "Abraham's Blessing" (below) to the tune of "She'll Be Coming 'Round the Mountain." Use your children's names ("Oh, Lisa and Jameel heard God say . . .") Remind the children that they are children of God.

Abraham's Blessing

1. Oh, ___ A - bra - ham and Sa - rah heard God say, Oh, ___
2. Oh, ___ I - saac and Re - be - kah heard God say, Oh, ___

A - bra - ham and Sa - rah heard God say, "I will
I - saac and Re - be - kah heard God say, "I will

love you and will bless you, I will love you and will bless you, I will
love you and will bless you, I will love you and will bless you, I will

love you and will bless you ev - ery day."
love you and will bless you ev - ery day."

WORDS: Beth Parr
MUSIC: Traditional
Words © 2001 Cokesbury, admin. by The Copyright Co., Nashville, TN
Sing to the tune of "She'll Be Coming 'Round the Mountain"

A Little Camel Music

Supplies: "A Little Camel Music" (CD), CD player

Before class mark a trail around the room with masking tape. Plan several stopping places. Teach the children how to bend over slightly and to do a jerky kind of walk as though they were riding camels.

Say: Let's pretend that we are Abraham and Sarah moving on our camels. When I play the music, camel-walk along the trail. When I stop the music, let's all sit on the floor in a circle and camp.

Bible Verse
God said,
"I will bless you."
Genesis 12:2, adapted

Play "A Little Camel Music" (CD). Let the children camel-walk along the trail. When you stop the music, have the children pretend to be cooking over a fire, eating around the fire, sleeping on their mats, and so forth.

Ask: Is God with us at our camping place? (*yes*)

Begin playing the music again and have the children continue camel-walking along the trail. Repeat the actions and the question every time you stop.

If your room is not large enough to accommodate a trail, plan to go out into the hall. If doing so is not possible, simply camel-walk in place.

CD
Track
❋ 5

23

Play a Game With Abraham

Supplies: "Abraham's Family" (page 25), CD, CD player

Sing this song as you play a game similar to "The Farmer in the Dell."

Have the children stand in a circle. Designate one child to be Abraham, who walks around the inside of the circle as the class sings the first verse.

On the second verse ask Abraham to choose another child (gender does not matter to very young children). Have Abraham and Sarah walk around the inside of the circle as you sing the second verse.

On the third verse have the children choose a third child to join them as Isaac.

On the fourth verse have the three children join hands and circle together. Then have them sit down in the center of the circle and choose a new Abraham.

Repeat until all children have had a chance to be in the center of the circle.

(Note: By the end of the song, most of the children will be sitting in the circle, and the "family" will be walking around them.)

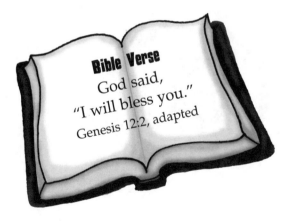

Bible Verse
God said,
"I will bless you."
Genesis 12:2, adapted

Abraham's Family

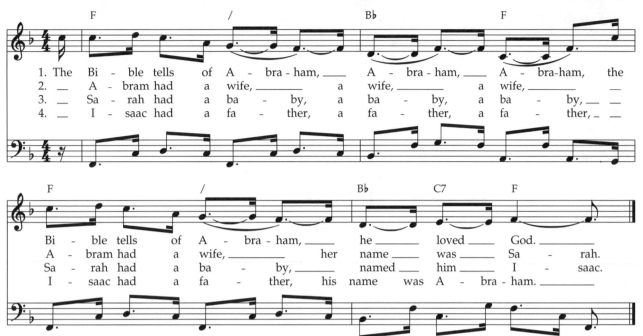

F / B♭ F

1. The Bi - ble tells of A - bra - ham, ___ A - bra - ham, ___ A - bra - ham, the
2. ___ A - bram had a wife, _____ a wife, _____ a wife, _____ ___
3. ___ Sa - rah had a ba - by, a ba - by, a ba - by, ___ ___
4. ___ I - saac had a fa - ther, a fa - ther, a fa - ther, ___ ___

F / B♭ C7 F

Bi - ble tells of A - bra - ham, ___ he ___ loved ___ God. ___
A - bram had a wife, _____ her name ___ was ___ Sa - rah.
Sa - rah had a ba - by, _____ named ___ him ___ I - saac.
I - saac had a fa - ther, his name was A - bra - ham. _____

WORDS: Evelyn M. Andre
MUSIC: Source unknown; arr. by Nylea L. Butler-Moore

CD Track #6

Sarah Laughed

Supplies: "Sarah Had a Baby Boy" (page 27), CD, CD player, baby doll

Have the children stand in a circle. Explain that you will give them a baby doll to pass around while you play music.

Say: When the music stops, the person who has the doll is Sarah. Sarah gets to laugh and laugh, but everyone else must be quiet.

Play "Sarah Had a Baby Boy." Stop the music often. The last time you stop the music, invite everyone to laugh with Sarah. (Note: to stop a song momentarily, push "Pause" and not "Stop")

Have the children lie down on the floor in a zigzag pattern. (One child lies down and the next child lies with his or her head on another child's stomach. Continue until all are in the line.)

Say: Now the first person will begin to say "Ha-Ha-Ha" and then as you hear the ha-ha-ha, begin to say, "Ha-Ha-Ha."

The children will all begin to laugh because of the funny feeling of their heads bouncing on each others' stomachs. Then have all the children sit up.

Say: Sarah laughed because she did not believe God would bless her with a baby boy. But God always keeps promises. Let's say a Bible verse: "God said, 'I will bless you.'"

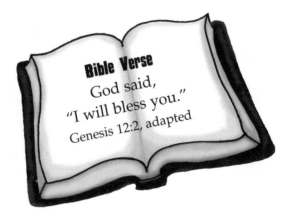

Bible Verse
God said,
"I will bless you."
Genesis 12:2, adapted

Sarah Had a Baby Boy

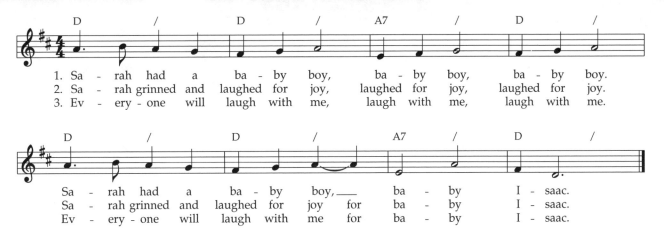

D / D / A7 / D /

1. Sa - rah had a ba - by boy, ba - by boy, ba - by boy.
2. Sa - rah grinned and laughed for joy, laughed for joy, laughed for joy.
3. Ev - ery-one will laugh with me, laugh with me, laugh with me.

D / D / A7 / D /

Sa - rah had a ba - by boy, ____ ba - by I - saac.
Sa - rah grinned and laughed for joy for ba - by I - saac.
Ev - ery-one will laugh with me for ba - by I - saac.

Actions: Pretend to rock baby, point to smile, Hold stomach, pretend to laugh.

WORDS: Sharilyn S. Adair
MUSIC: Traditional

CD Track #7

Jacob's Dream

Jacob Had a Dream

Supplies: "Jacob's Dream" (below)

This song is sung to the tune of "London Bridge." As you sing the first verse, have all the children get on the floor and pretend to be sleeping. As you sing the second verse, have all the children stand up and pretend to be climbing a ladder.

Bible Verse
God said, "Remember, I will be with you."
Genesis 28:15
Good News Translation

1. Ja - cob sleep - ing   on a rock,   on a rock,   on a rock.
2. Up and down the   an - gels climb,   an - gels climb,   an - gels climb.

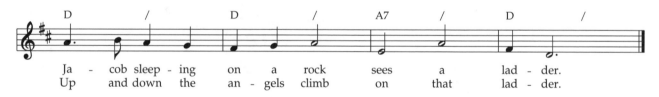

Ja - cob sleep - ing   on a rock   sees   a   lad - der.
Up and down the   an - gels climb   on   that   lad - der.

WORDS: Sharilyn S. Adair
MUSIC: Traditional

Words © 2001 Cokesbury, admin. by The Copyright Co., Nashville, TN

Sing to the tune of "London Bridge"

Sing and Remember

Supplies: "I Will Be With You" (below), CD, CD player

Learn the sign for *remember*: Gently fold your fingers over your palm, leaving your thumb resting next to your index finger. Bring the thumb of your right hand from the forehead down to touch the thumbnail of the left hand held in front of the chest, both palms facing down.

Play "I Will Be With You" (below) and ask the children to listen. Read the words of the song and ask the children to repeat them after you. Play the song again and invite the children to sing with you. Prompt them to sign the word "remember" each time it is sung. After singing, ask the children: "What do we remember?" (*that God is with us and will protect us wherever we go*). Repeat the song several times during the Sunday school lesson. At other times during the lesson, make the sign for *remember* and ask the children what it is that they are supposed to remember.

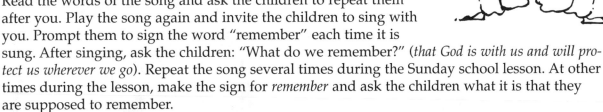

I will be with you wher - ev - er you go, re - mem - ber.____

I will pro - tect you wher - ev - er you go, re - mem - ber.____ And I will

bring you back to this land,____ re - mem - ber,____ re -

mem - ber,_____ re - mem - ber.____

WORDS: Genesis 28:15
MUSIC: June Fischer Armstrong

CD Track #8

29

Joseph

The Story of Joseph

Supplies: "Joseph" (below)

Use the following motions as you sing this song to the tune of "The Farmer in the Dell":

Verse 1: Hold arms out as if admiring a beautiful coat.
Verse 2: Stomp your feet and act mad.
Verse 3: Walk in place.
Verse 4: Pretend to place a crown on your head.
Verse 5: Pantomime handing out food.
Verse 6: Hug yourself.

Bible Verse
The LORD was with Joseph.
Genesis 39:2

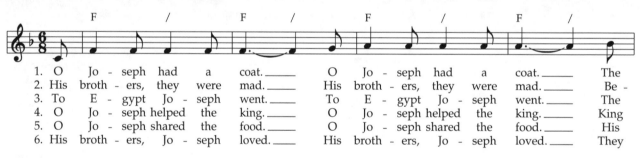

```
1. O    Jo - seph had    a    coat._____    O    Jo - seph had    a    coat._____    The
2. His  broth - ers, they were mad._____    His  broth - ers, they were mad._____    Be -
3. To   E - gypt Jo - seph went._____       To   E - gypt Jo - seph went._____       The
4. O    Jo - seph helped the  king._____    O    Jo - seph helped the  king._____    King
5. O    Jo - seph shared the  food._____    O    Jo - seph shared the  food._____    His
6. His  broth - ers, Jo - seph loved._____  His  broth - ers, Jo - seph loved._____  They
```

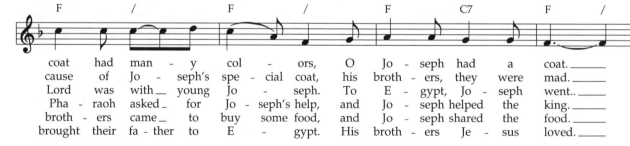

```
coat    had   man - y   col - ors,   O   Jo - seph had   a   coat._____
cause   of    Jo - seph's spe - cial coat, his broth - ers, they were mad._____
Lord    was   with_ young Jo - seph.  To  E - gypt, Jo - seph went.._____
Pha - raoh asked_ for  Jo - seph's help, and Jo - seph helped the king._____
broth - ers came_ to   buy   some food, and Jo - seph shared the food._____
brought their fa - ther to  E - gypt. His broth - ers Je - sus loved._____
```

WORDS: Daphna Flegal, based on Genesis 37:3, 28; 41:39-40; 42:25; 45:15)
MUSIC: Traditional

Words © 1997 Abingdon Press, admin. by The Copyright Co., Nashville, TN

Sing to the tune of *"The Farmer in the Dell"*

Where Is Joseph?

Encourage the children to do the motion as you lead them in the following story poem:

Where is Joseph? Oh, where can he be?
(*Place hand above eyes and look left and right.*)
Here I am. Can you see me?
(*Cover and uncover eyes with hands.*)
I'm wearing a wonderful coat from my father.
(*With arms bent at elbows, palms outward at shoulders, twist body left and right.*)
Can you see me? Can you see me?
(*Cover and uncover eyes with hands twice.*)

Where is Joseph? Oh, where can he be?
(*Place hand above eyes and look left and right.*)
Here I am. Can you see me?
(*Cover and uncover eyes with hands.*)
I'm riding a camel that's traveling to Egypt.
(*With elbows bent, hold hands in front as though holding reins.*
Repeat bending and straightening knees in a bounding movement.)
Can you see me? Can you see me?
(*Cover and uncover eyes with hands twice.*)

A Little Camel Music

Supplies: "A Little Camel Music" (CD), CD player

You may use this activity as a transition from arrival activities to your story time.

Say: In the Bible we read that Joseph took a long ride in a camel caravan. Let's be camels crossing the desert as we move to our story area.

Show the children how to bend slightly at the waist and to do a bumpy, jerky camel walk as you lead them around your classroom to the music of "A Little Camel Music." End up in your story area.

CD
Track
* 5

Baby Moses

Act Out the Story of Moses

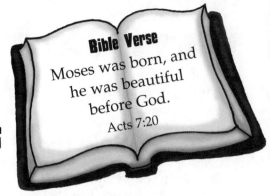

Bible Verse
Moses was born, and he was beautiful before God.
Acts 7:20

Supplies: "Where's Baby Moses?" (below)

Ask four children to pretend to be Moses, his mother, the princess, and Miriam. (Gender does not matter to young children, although five-year-old boys may begin to balk at pretending to be girls. If you do not make an issue of it, chances are the children will not, either.)

As you sing each verse of "Where's Baby Moses?" (below), ask the children to stand when you sing, "Here I am" and to pantomime the action listed in the song. (Sing this song to the tune of "Are You Sleeping?")

A Baby in the Water

Supplies: "Tiny Baby in the Water" (page 33), CD, CD player

Sing the song "Tiny Baby in the Water" (page 33) as an echo song. Sing the song a phrase at a time and ask the children to repeat after you. Or listen to the recording and ask the children to sing along with the children on the CD.

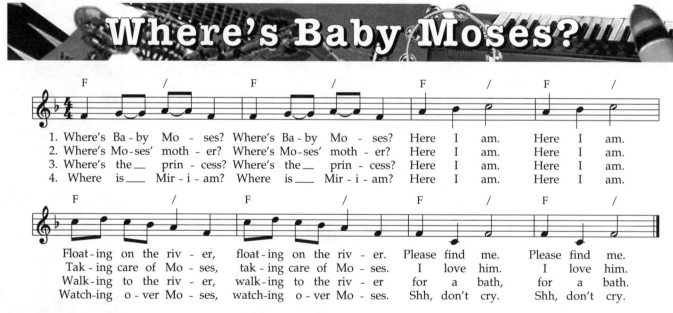

1. Where's Ba-by Mo-ses? Where's Ba-by Mo-ses? Here I am. Here I am.
2. Where's Mo-ses' moth-er? Where's Mo-ses' moth-er? Here I am. Here I am.
3. Where's the __ prin-cess? Where's the __ prin-cess? Here I am. Here I am.
4. Where is ___ Mir-i-am? Where is ___ Mir-i-am? Here I am. Here I am.

Float-ing on the riv-er, float-ing on the riv-er. Please find me. Please find me.
Tak-ing care of Mo-ses, tak-ing care of Mo-ses. I love him. I love him.
Walk-ing to the riv-er, walk-ing to the riv-er for a bath, for a bath.
Watch-ing o-ver Mo-ses, watch-ing o-ver Mo-ses. Shh, don't cry. Shh, don't cry.

WORDS: Sue Downing (based on Exodus 2:1-10)
MUSIC: Traditional

Sing to the tune of *"Are You Sleeping?"*

Tiny Baby in the Water

1. ① Mo - ses, (Mo - ses,) ② where are you hid - ing? (where are you hid - ing?)
2. ⑤ Prin - cess, (Prin - cess,) ⑥ found ba - by Mo - ses. (found ba - by Mo - ses.)
4. ⑨ Mo - ses, (Mo - ses,) ⑩ lived in the pal - ace. (lived in the pal - ace.)

Second time to Stanza 3
Third time - Fine

① Mo - ses, (Mo - ses,) ③ ti - ny __ ba - by in the ④ wa - ter.
⑤ Prin - cess, (Prin - cess,) ③ found ba - by Mo - ses in the ④ wa - ter.
⑨ Mo - ses, (Mo - ses,) ⑪ take your __ peo - ple out of E - gypt.

3. ⑦ Mi - ri - am, (Mi - ri - am,) ⑧ run get your moth - er. (run get your moth - er.)

D.C. al Fine

⑦ Mi - ri - am, (Mi - ri - am,) ③ bring her back for ba - by Mo - ses.

WORDS and MUSIC: Colleen Haley

CD Track #9

Rock Baby Moses

Supplies: "Little Baby Moses" (page 35), CD, CD player, baby doll, basket, soft blanket

Place a baby doll in a basket lined with a soft blanket. Have the children help make the bed soft enough for a baby. Quietly sing "Little Baby Moses" (page 35) while gently moving the basket back and forth on the floor.

Holy Moses Stomp

Supplies: "Holy Moses Stomp" (CD), CD player

Divide the children into two groups. Lead them in the "Holy Moses Stomp" on the CD.

Group 1: Baby Moses, where have you been?
Group 2: In a basket hiding from Pharaoh's men.
Group 1: Oh yeah? (*stomp, stomp*)
Group 2: Oh, yeah! (*stomp, stomp*)

Group 1: Grown up Moses, what is that sound?
Group 2: The crackle of flames on holy ground.
Group 1: Oh yeah? (*stomp, stomp*)
Group 2: Oh, yeah! (*stomp, stomp*)

Group 1: Stubborn Moses, what did God ask?
Group 2: For me to do an impossible task.
Group 1: Oh yeah? (*stomp, stomp*)
Group 2: Oh, yeah! (*stomp, stomp*)

Group 1: Leader Moses, what did you do?
Group 2: God parted the sea; I led them through.
Group 1: Oh yeah? (*stomp, stomp*)
Group 2: Oh, yeah! (*stomp, stomp*)

Group 1: Brother Moses, what do you see?
Group 2: My sister dancing because we are free.
Group 1: Oh yeah? (*stomp, stomp*)
Group 2: Oh, yeah! (*stomp, stomp*)

Group 1: Troubled Moses, what's all the fuss?
Group 2: My people are acting ridiculous.
Group 1: Oh yeah? (*stomp, stomp*)
Group 2: Oh, yeah! (*stomp, stomp*)

Group 1: Holy Moses, what have you got?
Group 2: Some rules from God that help a lot.
Group 1: Oh yeah? (*stomp, stomp*)
Group 2: Oh, yeah! (*stomp, stomp*)

Group 1: Holy Moses, what do you know?
Group 2: Following God is the way to go!
Group 1: Oh yeah? (*stomp, stomp*)
Group 2: Oh, yeah! (*stomp, stomp*)

CD Track #11

WORDS: Nancy Young and Joyce Brown
© 1996 Cokesbury

Little Baby Moses

Lit - tle ba - by Mo - ses, sleep, now, as you float,

rock - ing on the wa - ter in your lit - tle bas - ket boat.

WORDS and MUSIC: Joyce Riffe

CD Track #10

The Red Sea

CD Track #12

Moses Parts the Sea

Supplies: "Moses Parts the Red Sea" (CD), CD player

The simple structure of "Moses Parts the Red Sea" (CD) is a call and response. The leader reads the call, and the children respond by speaking and moving. Motions are suggested by the response. Each call and response is repeated one time. (If the leader is male, substitute "Yes, sir" for the response.)

Say: Imagine that you were a child in the days of Moses. You and your parents were in the band of Israelites hurrying out of Egypt.

Call: Did Moses strike the sea?
Response: Yes, ma'am.
Call: How did he do it?
Response: (*Child holds an imaginary staff and strikes up and down.*) Thump! Thump! Thump!

Call: Did you see the waters part?
Response: Yes, ma'am.
Call: How did they do it?
Response: (*Child holds back of hands together and moves them apart, out and back.*) Swish! Swish! Swish!

Call: Did you walk through the sea?
Response: Yes, ma'am.
Call: How did you go?
Response: (*Hands move up and down quickly slapping thighs.*) Run! Run! Run!

Call: Did the Egyptian soldiers come?
Response: Yes, ma'am.
Call: How did they come?
Response: (*March in place.*) March! March! March!

Call: Did the waters roll back?
Response: Yes, ma'am.
Call: How did they go?
Response: (*Make big, circular arm movements counterclockwise.*) Whoosh! Whoosh!

Bible Verse
Do not be afraid, stand firm.
Exodus 14:13

Call: Did you dance for joy?
Response: Yes, ma'am.
Call: How did you dance?
Response: (*Turn in circles, hands overhead.*) Twirl, Twirl.

Story adapted from *Grandmother Time Again*, © 1999 by Judy Gattis Smith.
Used by permission of the author.

Dance to "Sing and Celebrate!"

Supplies: "Sing and Celebrate" (below), CD, CD player, crepe paper strips, tape

Make crepe paper streamers by taping three or four lengths of crepe paper together. Invite the children to hold the taped end of the paper and to dance for joy to "Sing and Celebrate" (below) as the Israelites must have danced when they were delivered from the Egyptians.

Sing and Celebrate!

Sing and cel - e - brate! Sing and cel - e - brate! Make a joy-ful noise un - to___ the Lord!_

Sing and cel - e - brate! Sing and cel - e - brate! God is my sal - va - tion and song!_

God has done might - y things. God has set us free!
God is with me ev - ery day. God takes care of me!
God will give me what I need. I will trust in God!

WORDS and MUSIC: Colleen Haley
© 1996 Colleen Haley

CD Track #13

37

The Ten Commandments

Move to "The Ten Commandments

Supplies: "The Ten Commandments" (below)

Encourage the children to sing along and do the motions to "The Ten Commandments" (below). The song is sung to the tune of "Did You Ever See a Lassie?"

1. Do you know the Ten Com-mand-ments, Com-mand-ments, Com-mand-ments? Do you
(Show hands with ten fingers extended.)

know the Ten Com-mand-ments and that God loves you?
(Wrap arms around self in hug.)

2. Can you say the first Commandment, Commandment, Commandment?
   Can you say the first Commandment, that we will love God?
   (Cross hands over heart.)

3. O we can live together, together, together.
   O we can live together and follow God's laws.
   (Clap four times.)

WORDS: Elizabeth Crocker (based on Exodus 20:1-6)
MUSIC: Traditional

Words © 1996 Cokesbury, admin. by The Copyright Co., Nashville, TN

Sing to the tune of "Did You Ever See a Lassie?"

Bible Verse
God fills my life with good things.
Psalm 103:5, Good News Translation, adapted

Joshua, the Leader

Sing About Joshua

Supplies: "Joshua, Joshua" (below)

Teach the children the song "Joshua, Joshua" (below) to the tune of "Twinkle, Twinkle Little Star."

Clap and Stomp Litany

Tell the children that a litany is a way to praise God with words. Explain that you will say some words while clapping, and the children will respond with "Serve God!" as they stomp their feet twice. Say the children's words with them, showing them how to stomp their feet and extend their arms forward.

Joshua made a promise to
(*clap*)   (*clap*)
Serve God! (*Stomp feet and extend arms forward.*)
Joshua and his family would
(*clap*)   (*clap*)
Serve God! (*Stomp feet and extend arms forward.*)
Joshua asked the people to
(*clap*)   (*clap*)
Serve God! (*Stomp feet and extend arms forward.*)
And the people said they would
(*clap*)   (*clap*)
Serve God! (*Stomp feet and extend arms forward.*)

Bible Verse
We will serve the LORD.
Joshua 24:21

Joshua, Joshua

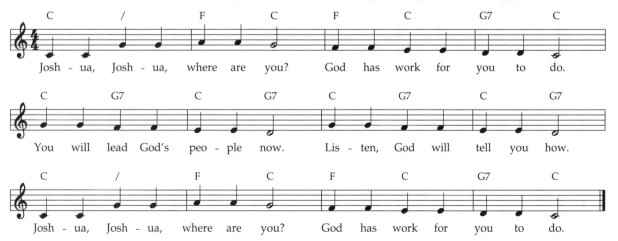

Josh-ua, Josh-ua, where are you? God has work for you to do.

You will lead God's peo-ple now. Lis-ten, God will tell you how.

Josh-ua, Josh-ua, where are you? God has work for you to do.

WORDS: Daphna Flegal
MUSIC: Traditional
Words © 1996 Cokesbury, admin. by The Copyright Co., Nashville, TN

Ruth and Naomi

Talking Thumbs

Supplies: "Ruth and Naomi" (below)

Show the children how to hold their fists in front of them and extend their thumbs up. They can have their thumbs "talk" to each other as they sing the song "Ruth and Naomi" (below). The song is sung to the tune of "Are You Sleeping?"

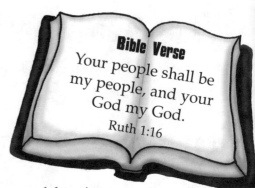

Where are you going? Where are you going? (*Bend right thumb up and down.*)
Ruth asked Naomi, Ruth asked Naomi. (*Bend right thumb up and down.*)
Going down to Bethlehem, going down to Bethlehem. (*Bend left thumb up and down.*)
To my home, to my home. (*Bend left thumb up and down.*)

I will go with you, I will go with you. (*Bend right thumb up and down.*)
Ruth told Naomi, Ruth told Naomi. (*Bend right thumb up and down.*)
I will go to Bethlehem, I will go to Bethlehem. (*Bend right thumb up and down.*)
To your home, to your home. (*Bend right thumb up and down.*)

1. Where are you go - ing? Where are you go - ing? Ruth asked Na - o - mi,
2. I will go with you, I will go with you, Ruth told Na - o - mi,

Ruth asked Na - o - mi. Go - ing down to Beth - le - hem,
Ruth told Na - o - mi. I will go to Beth - le - hem,

go - ing down to Beth - le - hem to my home, to my home.
I will go to Beth - le - hem to your home, to your home.

WORDS: Daphna Flegal
MUSIC: Traditional

Words © 1997 Abingdon Press, admin. by The Copyright Co., Nashville, TN

Sing to the tune of "Are You Sleeping?"

Samuel

Grow With Samuel

Supplies: "Little Samuel Grew" (page 42), CD, CD player

Show the children how to do the motions below as they sing "Little Samuel Grew" (page 42).

Inch by inch, day by day, little Samuel grew.
(*Start with hand close to floor, palm down and gradually move hand up.*)
Loving God, more and more. (*Hug yourself.*)
Just like you! (*Point to children.*)
When God called, (*Cup hands around mouth as if calling,*)
Sam said, "Yes! I'll serve you!" (*Nod head up and down.*)

Be a Helper Like Samuel

Supplies: "A Helper I Will Be" (page 43)

Sing "A Helper I Will Be" (page 43) to the tune of "The Farmer in the Dell." This song can be used to describe how Samuel helped Eli in the temple. It can also be used as a cleanup song. Sing the song as a signal that it is time to clean up the toys before story or snack time. Praise those who help. Since young children thrive on attention, they will soon all be helping in order to get you to praise them as well.

Samuel Hears God

Supplies: "Samuel! Samuel!" (page 43)

Let the children do the motions as you sing "Samuel" (page 43). (The song is sung to the tune of "Row, Row, Row Your Boat.")

Sam, Sam, Samuel," a voice called in the night
(*Cup hand around ears as if listening.*)
Samuel ran to Eli's room and called out, "Here am I."
(*Pat hands on thighs.*)

"Sam, Sam, Samuel, I did not call, my son.
(*Shake head back and forth.*)
I think the Lord is calling you, so go back and lie down."
(*Gesture away.*)

"Sam, Sam, Samuel," the voice came once again.
(*Cup hand around ears as if listening.*)
Samuel said, "Your servant hears," and heard God's message then.
(*Fold hands in lap.*)

Little Samuel Grew

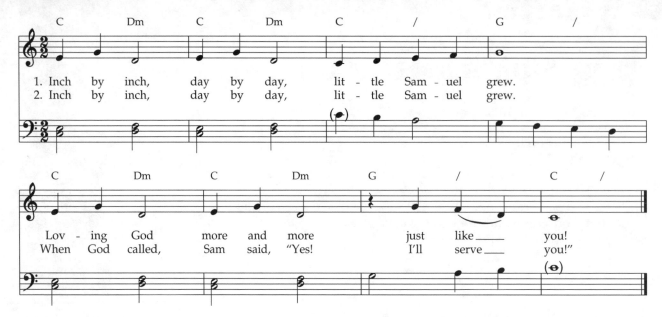

C   Dm   C   Dm   C   /   G   /

1. Inch by inch, day by day, lit – tle Sam – uel grew.
2. Inch by inch, day by day, lit – tle Sam – uel grew.

C   Dm   C   Dm   G   /   C   /

Lov – ing God more and more just like ____ you!
When God called, Sam said, "Yes! I'll serve ____ you!"

WORDS: James Ritchie
MUSIC: James Ritchie, arr. by Timothy Edmonds

CD Track #14

Bible Verse

And the boy Samuel grew up in the presence of the LORD.

1 Samuel 2:21b

A Helper I Will Be

1. A help-er I will be, a help-er I will be. There's
2. A help-er I will be, I'll put a-way my things. For

work to do, there's work to do, a help-er I will be.
I'm a lit-tle help-er, I'll put a-way my things!

WORDS: Source unknown
MUSIC: Traditional
Arr. © 1988 Graded Press, admin. by The Copyright Co., Nashville, TN

Samuel! Samuel!

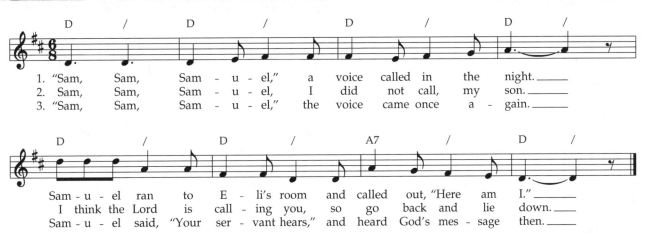

1. "Sam, Sam, Sam-u-el," a voice called in the night. _____
2. Sam, Sam, Sam-u-el, I did not call, my son. _____
3. "Sam, Sam, Sam-u-el," the voice came once a-gain. _____

Sam-u-el ran to E-li's room and called out, "Here am I." _____
I think the Lord is call-ing you, so go back and lie down. _____
Sam-u-el said, "Your ser-vant hears," and heard God's mes-sage then. _____

WORDS: Sharilyn S. Adair (based on 1 Samuel 3:1-10)
MUSIC: Traditional
Words © 1997 Abingdon Press, admin. by The Copyright Co., Nashville, TN

43

David, the Shepherd

Make a Harp

Supplies: "David Played the Harp" and "Play the Harp" (page 45), rubber bands; empty shoeboxes or tissue boxes; large metal cans, ruler; Y-shaped tree branches

Tell the children that today they are going to make harps to play, just as David played the harp when he was a shepherd boy.

Say: Harps can be made in many ways. All that is needed are some rubber bands and a way to stretch them!

The simplest harp is made by stretching rubber bands over an empty shoe box or tissue box. This resembles a guitar without a neck. Invite the children to experiment with the sounds that rubber bands of differing sizes make.

Another harp may be made by stretching rubber bands around a large metal can, such as a coffee can or extra large vegetable can. Make sure that the open can has no sharp edges that can hurt little fingers. Lay a six-inch ruler across the top of the can and stretch several rubber bands over it. See how turning the ruler on its side affects the sound of plucking the rubber bands.

A more authentic harp can be made by stretching rubber bands across the the branches of a Y-shaped tree branch. Notice how the pitch changes as the rubber bands are pulled tighter.

Bible Verse
I will praise you with the harp, O God, my God.
Psalm 43:4b

When the harps are finished, encourage them to play along and sing "David Played the Harp" and "Play the Harp" (page 45).

David Played the Harp

O Da - vid played the harp,_____ O Da - vid played the harp._____ He

sang songs of praise to God, O Da - vid played the harp._____

WORDS: Daphna Flegal
MUSIC: Traditional
Words © 1997 Abingdon Press, admin. by The Copyright Co., Nashville, TN

Sing to the tune of "The Farmer in the Dell"

Play the Harp

Play the harp. Play the harp. Sing a song of praise to God and play the harp.

WORDS: Daphna Flegal
MUSIC: Traditional
Words © 1997 Abingdon Press, admin. by The Copyright Co., Nashville, TN

Sing to the tune of "Hot Cross Buns"

David and Jonathan

Play a Friendship Game

Supplies: Bible storybook, "David and Jonathan" (below)

Tell the story of David and Jonathan from a Bible storybook. Then encourage the children to sing "David and Jonathan" (below) to the tune of "Are You Sleeping?"

Play a friendship game. Ask the children to sit in a circle. Point to two different children as you sing "Here is David, here is Jonathan." As you point to them, have the children stand up and hold hands.

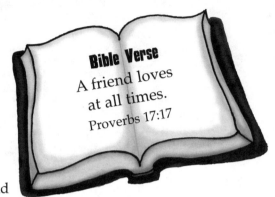

Bible Verse
A friend loves at all times.
Proverbs 17:17

As you sing the rest of the song, the two friends will walk, skip, or hop around the circle while holding hands. Then, they sit down. Sing the song again, choosing another David and Jonathan.

Here is Da - vid, Here is Jon - a - than. They are friends, they are friends.

They both made a prom - ise, they'd be friends for - ev - er. They are friends, they are friends.

WORDS: Sharilyn S. Adair and Daphna Flegal
MUSIC: Traditional

Words © 1997 Abingdon Press, admin. by The Copyright Co., Nashville, TN

Sing to the tune of "Are You Sleeping?"

Sign the Verse

Supplies: "A Friend Loves at All Times" (CD), CD player

Teach the children to sign the Bible verse. Then listen to "A Friend Loves at All Times" (CD) while signing the verse.

Friend — Hook the right index finger over the left index finger. Reverse.

Loves — Cross hands at wrists and press over your heart.

All - Hold the left palm toward the body. Circle the right hand out and around the left palm. End with the back of the right hand in the open left hand.

Times - Tap the back of the left hand with the right index finger.

CD Track #15

Psalms of Praise

Move to Psalm 150

Supplies: "Psalm 150" (page 49)

Let the children move to the song "Psalm 150" (page 49) to the tune of "Did You Ever See a Lassie?"

Bible Verse
Let everything that breathes praise the LORD!
Psalm 150:6a

Praise God

Supplies: "Praise God" (page 49), CD, CD player

Do the signs below as you sing the song "Praise God" (page 49):

Praise — Clap your hands several times.

God — Point the index finger of your right hand, with the other fingers curled down. Bring the hand down and open the palm.

Children — Hold one hand palm down. Pretend to pat the head of a child. Repeat several times as if patting several children.

Love — Cross hands at wrist and press over heart.

Thank — Touch fingertips to lips and then move hands down and back, one at a time.

Psalm 150

Praise the Lord and play the trum - pet, the trum - pet, the trum - pet. Praise the
(Pretend to play trumpet.)

Lord and play the trum - pet, the lute, and the harp.

2. Praise the Lord and start the dancing, the dancing, the dancing.
   (Sway back and forth.)
   Praise the Lord and start the dancing, the strings, and the pipe!

3. Praise the Lord and play the cymbals, the cymbals, the cymbals.
   (Pretend to play the cymbals.)
   Praise the Lord and play the cymbals, and the tambourine, too.

4. O let everything that's breathing, that's breathing, that's breathing.
   (Turn around.)
   O let everything that's breathing sing praise to the Lord!

WORDS: Linda Ray Miller, Sharilyn S. Adair, and Daphna Flegal (based on Psalm 150)
MUSIC: Traditional

Sing to the tune of "Did You Ever See a Lassie?"

CD Track #18

Praise God

Praise God, praise God, all you lit - tle chil - dren, God is love, God is love.

Praise God, praise God, all you lit - tle chil - dren, God is love, God is love.

WORDS and MUSIC: Traditional

Wiggle Praise

I *wig - gle, wig - gle, wig - gle, and I praise the Lord! _ I

wig - gle, wig - gle, wig - gle, and I praise the Lord! _ I

wig - gle, wig - gle, wig - gle, and I praise the Lord! _ Al - le - lu - ia!

*Additional stanzas: jump, stomp, clap.

WORDS and MUSIC: Linda Ray Miller and Daphna Flegal

© 2000 Cokesbury, admin. by The Copyright Co., Nashville, TN

CD
Track
#17

Bible Verse
I will praise the Lord
as long as I live.
Psalm 146:2a

Clap Your Hands

Clap your hands, (clap, clap, clap) all you peo-ples; (clap, clap, clap) and shout to God with loud songs of joy. (Shout hoo-ray.) Clap your hands (clap, clap, clap) for the Bi-ble, (clap, clap, clap) God's spe-cial gift to ev-ery girl and boy. (Shout hoo-ray.)

WORDS: Sharilyn S. Adair
MUSIC: Timothy Edmonds

CD Track #16

Prophets

Learn About Jeremiah

Supplies: "Jeremiah's Call" (page 53)

Help the children know that God calls children to be prophets. Remind the children of the story of Jeremiah being called by God, and how Jesus knew that he was God's son even when he was a just a boy.

Let the children enjoy singing "Jeremiah's Call" (page 53).

We Can Speak for God

Supplies: "The Prophets" (page 53)

Teach the children that a prophet is one who speaks for God.

   Say: Any one of us can be a prophet if we listen to God's word and tell it to others.

Lead the children in singing and moving to "The Prophets" (page 53).

Bible Verse
You shall speak whatever I command you.
Jeremiah 1:7c

Jeremiah's Call

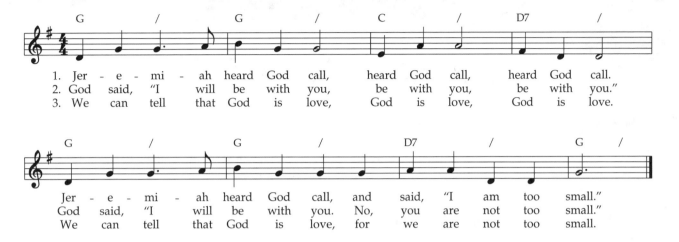

| G | / | G | / | C | / | D7 | / |

1. Jer – e – mi – ah heard God call, heard God call, heard God call.
2. God said, "I will be with you, be with you, be with you."
3. We can tell that God is love, God is love, God is love.

| G | / | G | / | D7 | / | G | / |

Jer – e – mi – ah heard God call, and said, "I am too small."
God said, "I will be with you. No, you are not too small."
We can tell that God is love, for we are not too small.

WORDS: Beth Parr
MUSIC: Traditional
Words © 2001 Cokesbury, admin. by The Copyright Co., Nashville, TN

Sing to the tune of "Do You Know the Muffin Man?"

The Prophets

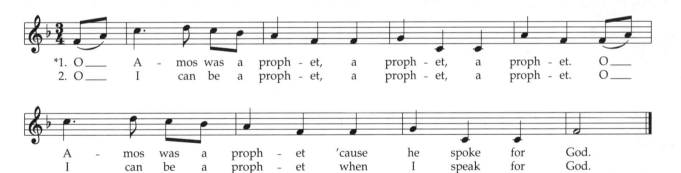

*1. O___ A – mos was a proph – et, a proph – et, a proph – et. O___
2. O___ I can be a proph – et, a proph – et, a proph – et. O___

A – mos was a proph – et 'cause he spoke for God.
I can be a proph – et when I speak for God.

*Add verses using other names of prophets: Elijah, Elisha, Hosea, Jeremiah, Ezekiel, Isaiah, Huldah)

WORDS: Linda Ray Miller
MUSIC: Traditional
Words © 1997 Abingdon Press, admin. by The Copyright Co., Nashville, TN

Sing to the tune of "Did You Ever See a Lassie?"

Queen Esther

Sing About Queen Esther

Supplies: "Let Us Sing About Queen Esther" (page 55)

Let the children enjoy the song "Let Us Sing About Queen Esther" (page 55) to the tune of "Did You Ever See a Lassie?"

Follow Me

Supplies: crown

Choose a child to be Queen Esther. Place a crown on the child's head, if you have one. Hold the child's hand and lead the children around the room in a "Follow the Leader" game. Wind the children around the room, circling chairs and tables to make the game more fun. Change how you move (walk, hop, tiptoe, march) and have the children copy your movements. As you move around the room, sing "Follow Me" to the tune of "London Bridge."

Follow me, for I am queen,
I am queen, I am queen.
Follow me, for I am queen.
I help my people.
(*Stand still and wave like a beauty queen.*)

If you have a small number of children, sing the song several times. After each time that you stop and wave, choose a different child to be Queen Esther.

If you have a large number of children and do not have time for everyone to have a turn, play the game and be Queen Esther yourself.

When you finish the game, have everyone sit down in the story area.

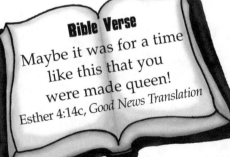

Bible Verse
Maybe it was for a time like this that you were made queen!
Esther 4:14c, *Good News Translation*

54

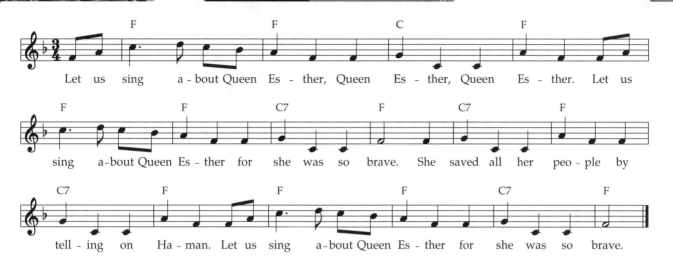

Let Us Sing About Queen Esther

Let us sing a-bout Queen Es – ther, Queen Es – ther, Queen Es – ther. Let us

sing a-bout Queen Es – ther for she was so brave. She saved all her peo – ple by

tell – ing on Ha – man. Let us sing a-bout Queen Es – ther for she was so brave.

WORDS: Sharilyn S. Adair
MUSIC: Traditional
Words © 1997 Abingdon Press, admin. by The Copyright Co., Nashville, TN

Sing to the tune of "Did You Ever See a Lassie?"

Daniel

Make a Lion's Mask

Supplies: "Lion Music" (CD), CD player, lion's mask (page 57), scissors, glue, paper plates, crayons or markers, yarn, craft sticks

Photocopy the lion's mask on page 57 for each student. Cut out the masks and glue them onto a paper plate. Let the children color the lion's mask. Show the children how to place glue around the edges of the plates. Then let them glue pieces of yarn around the edges to make the lion's mane. When each child completes the lion face, tape or glue a large craft stick to the bottom of the mask. Show the children how to use the masks holding the masks to their faces.

Ask one child to pretend to be Daniel and kneel in prayer. The other children may be lions and can circle Daniel, but cannot touch him, because God is protecting Daniel.

Encourage further dramatic play as lions by playing "Lion Music" on the CD. Ask the children to move like lions as they listen to the music.

1. O Dan - iel prayed to God,_____ O Dan - iel prayed to God. _____ They
2. But God kept Dan - iel safe,_____ but God kept Dan - iel safe._____

threw him in the li - on's den be - cause he prayed to God. _____
E - ven in the li - on's den, his God kept Dan - iel safe. _____

WORDS: Daphna Flegal and Sharilyn S. Adair
MUSIC: Traditional
Words © 1997 Abingdon Press, admin. by The Copyright Co., Nashville, TN

Bible Verse
Let us choose what is right.
Job 34:4

Nehemiah

Gonna Build a Wall

Supplies: "Gonna Build a Wall" (CD), CD player, blocks

As you learn the story of Nehemiah, help the children see that it was only through working together that Nehemiah and his friends were able to finish the wall. Listen to "Gonna Build a Wall" (CD) as you build a wall out of blocks with everyone participating in the building.

Gonna build a wall! (*echo*)
Gonna build it high! (*echo*)
Gonna build it up, up, up (*echo*)
Into the sky! (*echo*)

Gonna build it tall. (*echo*)
Gonna build it strong. (*echo*)
Gonna build it tall and very strong (*echo*)
To last my whole life long. (*echo*)

Walls are made of many stones (*echo*)
Many kinds of different stones (*echo*)
Big stones, little stones (*echo*)
Very, very small stones. (*echo*)

Gonna build a wall! (*echo*)
Gonna build it high! (*echo*)
Gonna build it up, up, up (*echo*)
Into the sky! (*echo*)

Gonna build it tall. (*echo*)
Gonna build it strong. (*echo*)
Gonna build it tall and very strong, (*echo*)
To last my whole life long. (*echo*)

CD Track #20

Bible Verse
For we are partners working together for God.
1 Corinthians 3:9,
Good News Translation

The Birth of Jesus

Clippity Clop Like a Donkey

Supplies: "Clippity Clop" (below), CD, CD player, paper cups, markers, crepe paper strips, glue or tape

Give each child two paper cups. Let the children decorate their paper cups with markers. Give each child several crepe paper streamers to attach to the bottom of each cup with glue or tape.

Say: These are called "clip clops." You can use them to praise God by waving the streamers in the air, or you can clop them together to make the sound a donkey's hooves make. Let's praise God for baby Jesus.

Have the children hold their clip clops and sit in a circle on the floor. Play "Clippity Clop"(below) and have the children wave their streamers in the air or clop their cups together as the music plays.

WORDS and MUSIC: Diana Flegal and Daphna Flegal

© 1992 Cokesbury, admin. by The Copyright Co., Nashville, TN

CD Track #21

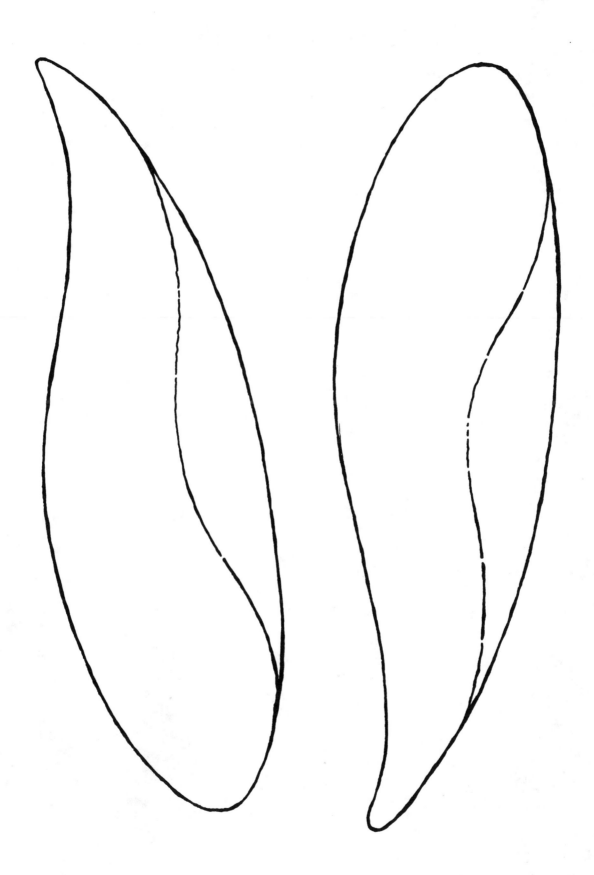

Make Praise Instruments

Supplies: "Angel Band" (page 63), CD, CD player; plastic one-liter soda bottles, small plastic beads or aquarium gravel, bright primary colors of masking tape, electrical tape; paper plates, markers, masking tape, stapler and staples, small buttons or beads, crepe paper streamers; empty coffee cans with plastic lids, wrapping paper, markers, tape or glue, two unsharpened pencils, large wooden beads; sticks, dowels, or unsharpened pencils

Make several of the rhythm instruments below. Make sure that each child has an instrument to play. Ask the children to sit in a circle with their instruments on their laps. As you sing the verse ("There was one, there were two…), have the children hold up fingers indicating the number of angels. As you get to the refrain ("Oh, wasn't that a band"), have the children pick up their instruments and play them. At the end of the refrain all instruments return to laps.

Make a Bead Rattle: Pour about one cup of beads or gravel into the soda bottle. Using bright colors of tape, cover the top half of the bottle with masking tape. Then use brightly-colored electrical tape to cover up the loose ends of the masking tape as shown. Shake and enjoy.

Make a Tambourine: Decorate the outside of a paper plate. Staple crepe paper streamers to the edges of the pan or plate. Place a few buttons or beads inside the plate and fold it in half. Staple and/or tape the edges of the plate together so that the buttons and beads stay on the inside of the plate.

Make a Drum: Decorate the coffee cans by measuring and gluing a piece of wrapping paper around the can. Tape or glue a wooden bead to one end of each pencil drumstick.

Rhythm Sticks: Beat two sticks, dowels, or unsharpened pencils together in rhythm to the song.

The Angel Band

There was one, there were two, there were three lit - tle an - gels, there were

four, there were five, there were six lit - tle an - gels, there were

sev - en, there were eight, there were nine lit - tle an - gels,

ten lit - tle ___ an - gels in the band. _____ Oh,

was - n't that a band, Christ - mas morn - ing, Christ - mas

morn - ing, Christ - mas morn - ing! Was - n't that a band,

Christ - mas morn - ing, Christ - mas morn - ing soon! _____

WORDS and MUSIC: Traditional

63

Rock the Baby

Supplies: "Little Jesus" (below), CD, CD player, paper plates, tape, large craft sticks, marker (optional: happy face stickers)

Give each child a paper plate. Help the child fold the bottom of the paper plate up about an inch. Fold both sides of the plate to the middle, leaving the top open (so that the plate looks like a burrito). Tape the sides of the plate in place. Now give each child a large craft stick on which you have drawn a face. Place the craft stick into the paper plate so that the face "peeks out" between the folds. Or, find large "happy face" stickers and place the stickers at the top of the plates.

Say: You have made a baby Jesus doll, all wrapped up in swaddling cloths! Let's sing him a lullaby and rock him to sleep.

Sing the song "Little Jesus" with the children. Encourage the children to "rock" their babies to the lull-aby. Or let the children pretend to rock babies if you choose not to make the baby Jesus dolls.

1. Lit - tle Je - sus, sleep in the hay; lit - tle Je - sus, too small to play.
2. Lit - tle Je - sus, sleep in the hay; lit - tle Je - sus, too small to play.

Mar - y sing - ing, Jo - seph near - by; who will see your star in the sky?
Lit - tle Je - sus, soon you'll grow tall; you'll be show - ing God's love to all.

WORDS: Bob J. Golter, Sam S. Barefield, Evelyn M. Andre
MUSIC: Bob J. Golter; harm. by V. Earle Copes

CD Track #25

Friendly Beast Puppets

Supplies: "The Friendly Beasts (page 66), CD, CD player, puppet heads (pages 68–71), card stock, scissors, glue or tape, thin paper plates or large craft sticks, crayons or markers

Photocopy the puppet heads on pages 68–71. Make sure each child has a puppet head. Ask the children to decorate their puppet heads. If you like, you may copy the puppet heads onto card stock and ask an adult helper to cut out the eye holes. Or glue the decorated puppet heads to a thin paper plate. Glue or tape a large craft stick for a handle.

Let the children listen to "The Friendly Beasts" (page 66) on the CD. Have the children hold their puppets behind their backs as they listen to the first verse. On the second verse, ask the children who are holding donkey puppets to bring out their puppets and let them "sing." All other puppets should remain behind the children's backs. On the third verse, the donkey puppets go behind the backs, and the children holding cow puppets may bring theirs out to "sing." On the fourth verse, the sheep puppets sing, and on the fifth verse, the dove. On the sixth verse, let all the puppets come out to sing.

Donkey Music

Supplies: "Donkey Music" (CD), CD player, construction paper, scissors, donkey ears (page 61), tape or stapler and staples

CD Track #22

Give each child a paper headband cut from construction paper and a pair of donkey ears (photocopied) on page 61. Help the children tape the ears onto the headbands. Tape or staple each child's headband to fit around his or her head. Play "Donkey Music." Let the children pretend to be donkeys and move to the music.

Sing a Familiar Song

Supplies: "Away in a Manger" (page 67), CD, CD player

Use the following motions for this familiar carol:

Away in a manger
(*Place hand on forehead, palm down as if looking away.*)
no crib for a bed.
(*Wave index finger back and forth while shaking your head no.*)
The little Lord Jesus lay down his sweet head.
(*Place palms together; lay your head against your hands as if sleeping.*)
The stars in the sky
(*Point up to the sky.*)
looked down where he lay.
(*Point down to the floor.*)
The little Lord Jesus, asleep on the hay.
(*Place palms together; lay your head against your hands as if sleeping.*)

The Friendly Beasts

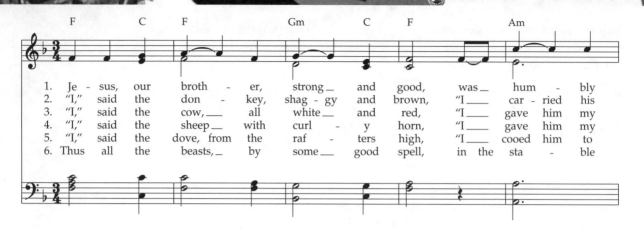

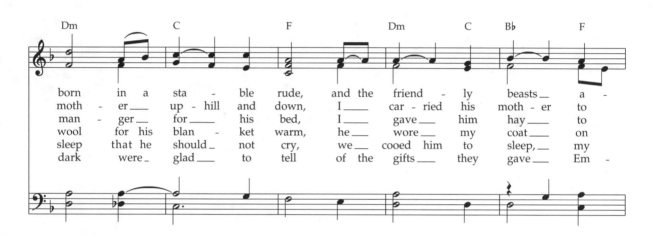

1. Je - sus, our broth - er, strong and good, was hum - bly
2. "I," said the don - key, shag - gy and brown, "I car - ried his
3. "I," said the cow, all white and red, "I gave him my
4. "I," said the sheep with curl - y horn, "I gave him my
5. "I," said the dove, from the raf - ters high, "I cooed him to
6. Thus all the beasts, by some good spell, in the sta - ble

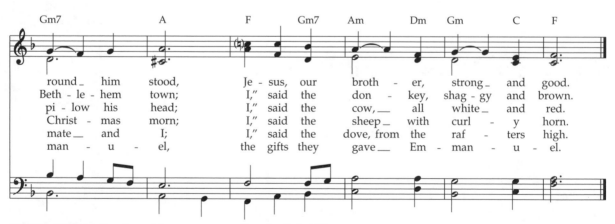

born in a sta - ble rude, and the friend - ly beasts a -
moth - er up - hill and down, I car - ried his moth - er to
man - ger for his bed, I gave him hay to
wool for his blan - ket warm, he wore my coat on
sleep that he should not cry, we cooed him to sleep, my
dark were glad to tell of the gifts they gave Em -

round him stood, Je - sus, our broth - er, strong and good.
Beth - le - hem town; I," said the don - key, shag - gy and brown.
pi - low his head; I," said the cow, all white and red.
Christ - mas morn; I," said the sheep with curl - y horn.
mate and I; I," said the dove, from the raf - ters high.
man - u - el, the gifts they gave Em - man - u - el.

WORDS: 12th cent. French carol; trans. anonymous (based on Luke 2:7)
MUSIC: Medieval French melody; harm. by Carlton R. Young

CD Track #26

66

Away in a Manger

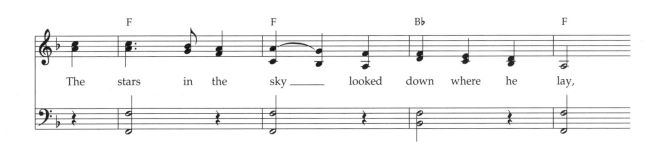

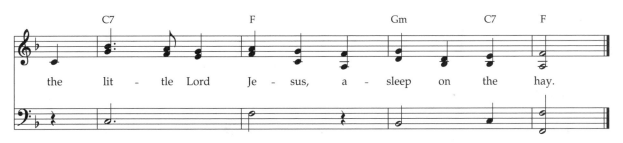

WORDS: Anon. (based on Luke 2:7)
MUSIC: James R. Murray

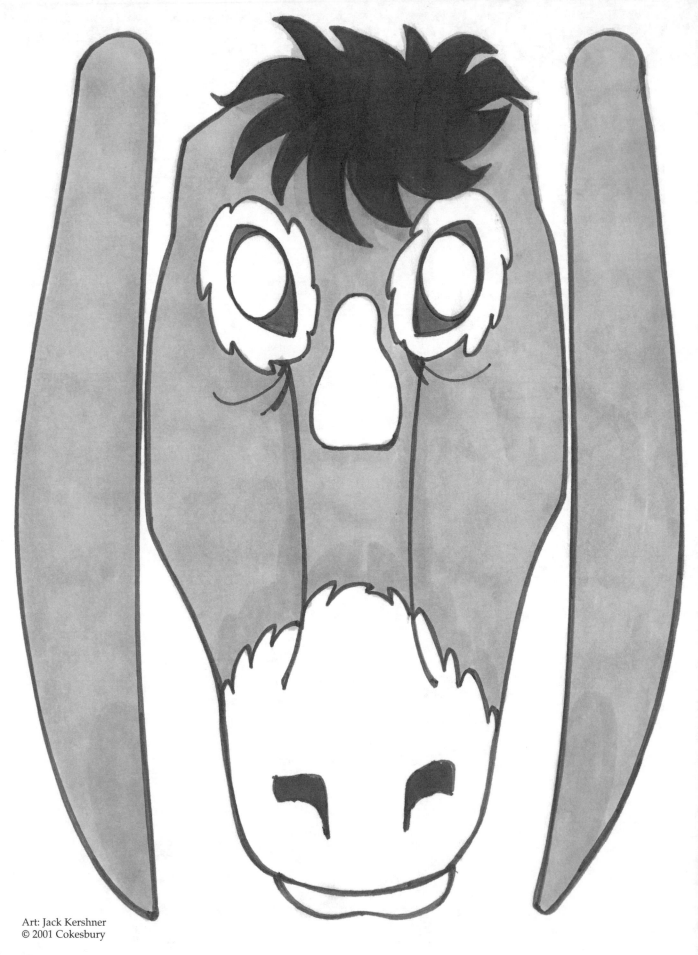

Art: Jack Kershner
© 2001 Cokesbury

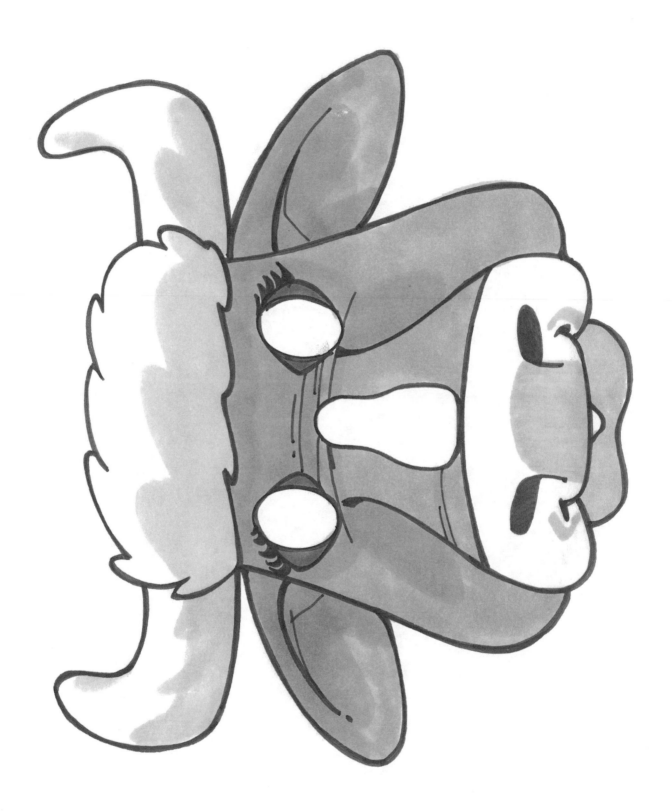

69

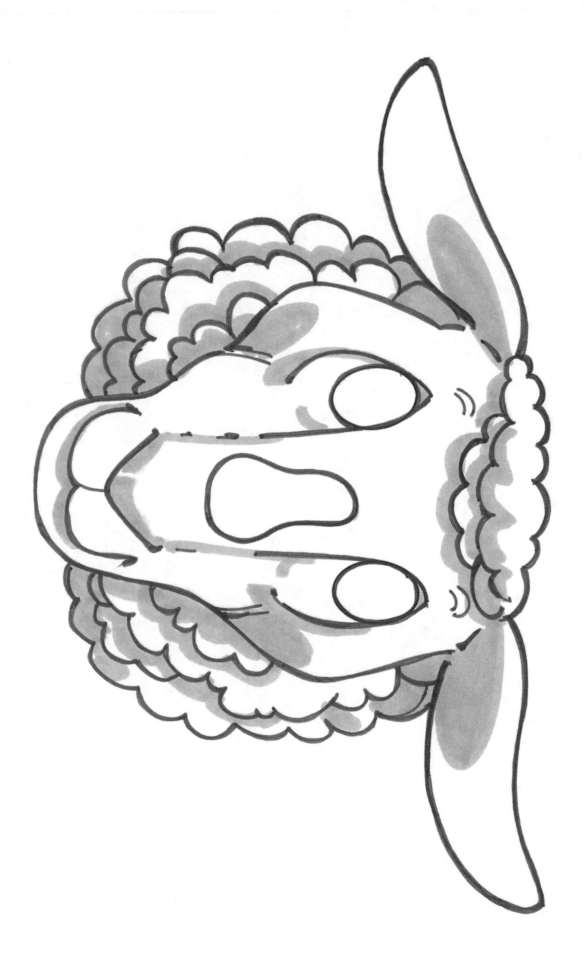

The Wise Men

Wise Men Travel

Lead the children in the suggested motions as you tell the story of the wise men searching for Jesus. Encourage the children to say the phrase "That is good news!" with you.

Look! Look! Look! (*Point up.*)
The wise men saw a bright star shining in the sky.
That is good news!

Clop! Clop! Clop! (*Pat your legs.*)
The wise men rode their camels for many, many days.
They followed the star to Bethlehem.
That is good news!

Twinkle! Twinkle! Twinkle! (*Sign the word* twinkle.)
The star led the wise men to Jesus.
That is good news!

Kneel, Kneel, Kneel. (*Bend your knees.*)
The wise men knelt down and gave Jesus special gifts.
That is good news!

Praise! Praise! Praise! (*Clap your hands.*)
The wise men praised God for Jesus.
That is good news!

twinkle

Star Music

Supplies: "Star Music" (CD), CD player, aluminum foil or gold gift wrap

Tell the children the story of the wise men coming across the desert to see the new King.

Make a large star out of aluminum foil or gold foil gift wrap. Ask one child to carry the star and lead the other children around the room while you listen to "Star Music." Encourage the children to move as if they were riding camels.

CD Track *27

Twinkle, Twinkle, Shining Star

Twin - kle, twin - kle shin - ing star, guid - ing wise men from a - far

to a home so far a - way, where lit - tle Je - sus played all day.

Twin - kle, twin - kle, shin - ing star, guid - ing wise men from a - far.

WORDS: Sue Downing
MUSIC: Traditional
Words © 1990 Graded Press, admin. by The Copyright Co., Nashville, TN

Sing to the tune of "Twinkle, Twinkle Little Star"

Amen Aerobics

Supplies: "Amen" (below), CD, CD player

Play "Amen" for the children. Have all the children do the following motions on the amens:

First stanza: Clap hands.
Second stanza: Snap fingers (or tap thumb and middle finger together).
Third stanza: Stomp feet.

Divide the class into three groups. Tell the children that the first group will clap its hands, the second group will snap its fingers, and the third group will stomp its feet on the amens for all the stanzas. Play the song and have the groups do their assigned motions at the same time.

For a more strenuous version of "Amen," have the children stand in a circle. Have the children do the following motions to the amens.

A-men: Stand up and hold arms above head. Shake hands and bring arms down as you squat and touch the floor.
A-men: Stand up and hold arms above head. Shake hands and bring arms down as you squat and touch the floor.
A-men: Stand up and hold arms above head. Shake hands and bring arms down as you squat and touch the floor.
Amen: Stand up and stomp one foot. Stomp the other foot.
Amen: Clap hands twice.

*All voices may repeat the first "Amens" after stanza 3.

WORDS: African American spiritual
MUSIC: African American spiritual; harm. by J. Jefferson Cleveland and Verolga Nix; adapt. by Nylea L. Butler-Moore
Harm © 1981 Abingdon Press; adapt. © 1993 Abingdon Press, admin. by The Copyright Co., Nashville, TN

Jesus Grew

Move to a Poem

Say the poem below for the children. Encourage them to say the words and do the motions after you.

Jesus learned things as he grew. (*Crouch down, then stand up.*)
Just like me, (*Point to self.*)
And just like you! (*Point to others.*)
He learned to walk, (*Walk in place.*)
And run and jump, (*Run in place; jump in place.*)
He learned to stand up tall. (*Stretch up on tiptoes, arms raised above head.*)
He learned to talk, (*Point to mouth.*)
And laugh (*Fold arms over stomach and shake arms as if laughing.*)
and sing. (*Cup hands around mouth.*)
He learned God loves us all. (*Hug self.*)
God loved Jesus as he grew. (*Crouch down, then stand up.*)
Just like me, (*Point to self.*)
And just like you! (*Point to others.*)

Ask: What are some of the things you can do?

Grow With Jesus

Say the poem below for the children. Encourage them to say the words and do the motions after you.

Jesus grew from a baby,
(*Rock baby in your arms.*)
Just like me and you.
(*Point to self; point to others.*)
He learned to walk.
(*Walk in place.*)
He learned to talk.
(*Cup hands around mouth.*)
He grew and grew and grew!
(*Crouch down, then stretch up slowly to tiptoes with arms overhead.*)

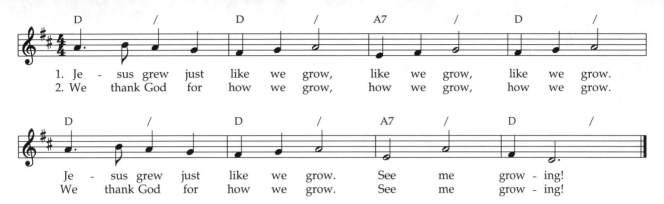

Jesus Grew

| D | / | D | / | A7 | / | D | / |

1. Je - sus grew just like we grow, like we grow, like we grow.
2. We thank God for how we grow, how we grow, how we grow.

| D | / | D | / | A7 | / | D | / |

Je - sus grew just like we grow. See me grow - ing!
We thank God for how we grow. See me grow - ing!

WORDS: Daphna Flegal
MUSIC: Traditional

Words © 1996 Cokesbury, admin. by The Copyright Co., Nashville, TN

Sing to the tune of "London Bridge"

Bible Verse

The child grew and became strong

Luke 2:40a

Good News Translation

Jesus in the Temple

Going to the Temple

Lead the children to your story area with the following song, sung to the tune of "London Bridge."

We're walking to the Temple now,
(*Walk around room.*)
Temple now, Temple now.
We're walking to the Temple now.
See us walking!

We're hopping to the Temple now,
(*Hop around room.*)
Temple now, Temple now.
We're hopping to the Temple now.
See us hopping!

We're marching to the Temple now,
(*March around room.*)
Temple now, Temple now.
We're marching to the Temple now.
See us marching!

Bible Verse
And all who heard him were amazed at his understanding.
Luke 2:47a

Learning About God

Supplies: Bible

Lead the children in the following litany after hearing the story of Jesus in the Temple.

Teacher: At home with Mary and Joseph,
Children: Jesus learned about God.

Teacher: With the teachers in the Temple,
Children: Jesus learned about God.

Teacher: As he listened and asked questions,
Children: Jesus learned about God.

Jesus Learned About God

WORDS: Millie Goodson
MUSIC: Millie Goodson; arr. by Nylea L. Butler-Moore

Jesus' Baptism

In The River

Tell the children that you want them to help you retell the Bible story. Say the chorus, "In the river, in the water, River Jordan, that is." Repeat this several times with a steady rhythm. Clap when you say the words *river*, *water*, *Jordan*, and *is*, for a total of four claps. Practice the chorus with the children. Then read the poem. Have the children clap and say the chorus with you each time.

Down by the water, Jesus found John.
In the river, in the water,
River Jordan, that is.
Baptizing people one by one.
In the river, in the water,
River Jordan, that is.
Jesus said, "John, baptize me!"
In the river, in the water,
River Jordan, that is.
"That's how God wants things to be."
In the river, in the water,
River Jordan, that is.
Jesus was baptized there by John.
In the river, in the water,
River Jordan, that is.
God said, "This is my own, dear Son."
In the river, in the water,
River Jordan, that is.
The Spirit of God came like a dove.
In the river, in the water,
River Jordan, that is.
Jesus knew of God's great love.
In the river, in the water,
River Jordan, that is.

Dance to "Drip, Drop"

Supplies: "Drip, Drop, Splish, Splash" (page 81), CD, CD player, blue, green, and white crepe paper

Make water streamers out of blue, green, and white crepe paper and let the children dance as they listen to the music. Talk with the children about the ways we use water. Tell the children that they can pretend their streamers are waves of water. When they wave their arms, the water will move. Encourage the children to wave their arms in big, sweeping motions to make large waves. Have them make small circle motions to make ripples of water.

Drip, Drop, Splish, Splash

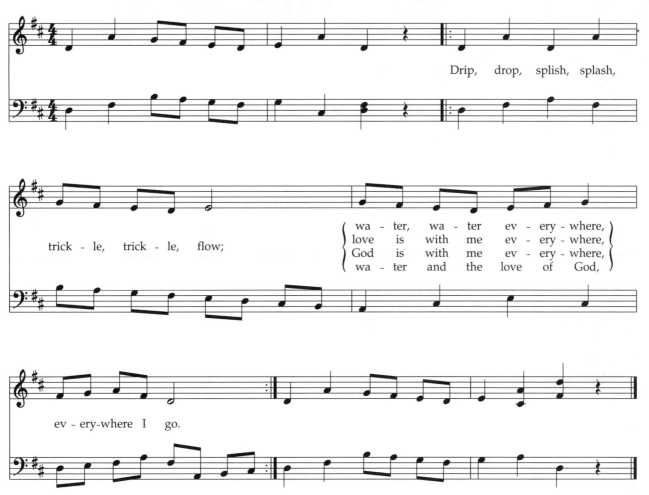

Drip, drop, splish, splash, trick - le, trick - le, flow;

wa - ter, wa - ter ev - ery - where,
love is with me ev - ery - where,
God is with me ev - ery - where,
wa - ter and the love of God,

ev - ery-where I go.

WORDS and MUSIC: James Ritchie

CD Track #30

Jesus Teaches

What Jesus Said

Lead the children in the motions as you say the following poem:

I stretch my fingers way up high.
(*Reach up to the ceiling with fingertips as far as you can.*)
I reach from side to side.
(*Extend arms side to side.*)
I'll give myself a great big hug.
(*Wrap arms across your chest with a hugging motion.*)
There's so much love inside.
(*Continue hugging. Sway from side to side.*)

The God who made me put it there.
(*Point to heart.*)
God put it there for me to share.
(*Point to heart, then extend hands forward, palms up.*)
I'll give my love to God and you.
(*Trace a big heart in the air.*)
That's what Jesus said to do.
(*Nod head as if saying yes.*)

Five Happy Children

Have the children hold up their hands and wiggle their fingers. Tell them
they are going to use their fingers to help tell the Bible story today.
Encourage the children to do the motions as you tell them the fingerplay.

(*Hold up hand and wiggle fingers.*)
Five happy children went to church one day,
Where they learned about God's love and here is what they say:
(*Hold up one finger.*)
This one said: "Love God with all your heart."
(*Hold up two fingers.*)
This one said: "Love God with all your soul."
(*Hold up three fingers.*)
This one said: "Love God with all your strength."
(*Hold up four fingers.*)
This one said: "Love God with all your mind."
(*Hold up five fingers.*)
This one said: "And your neighbor as yourself."
(*Wiggle finger.s.*)
Five happy children thought of Jesus long ago,
How he taught of God's love so that we could know.

Make and Play Instruments

Supplies: "If I Had a Drum" (below), CD, CD player, rhythm instruments

Use rhythm instruments and play along with "If I Had a Drum" (below) on the CD. Make a drum out of a coffee can or round oatmeal canister, or make a decorated drum (page 62). See page 44 for instructions on making a harp. Use a drinking straw for a flute. For a large class, divide into three groups and have each group take a different instrument. The children are to play only on their own verse. Everyone sings or signs the final verse.

Sign and Sing About Love

Supplies: "Jesus Loves Me" (page 84), "Love One Another" (page 85), CD, CD player

Teach the signs for the refrain of "Jesus Loves Me" (page 84). Have the children sign the refrain as they sing the song. Then teach the children the sign language for *love one another*. Help them sign the phrase as you play "Love One Another" (page 85) on the CD.

If I Had a Drum

1. If I had a drum, I'd drum a song of Je - sus,
2. If I had a harp, I'd strum a song of Je - sus,
3. If I had a flute, I'd blow a song of Je - sus,
4. I can use my hands to sign a song of Je - sus,

tell - ing of his

love, and how he helped the peo - ple.

Pum, pum, pum, pum, pum, pum.
Strum, strum, strum, strum, strum, strum.
Foo, foo, foo, foo, foo, foo.
(sign "Jesus loves you.")

WORDS: E. S. Jennings
MUSIC: J. R. Jennings

© 1984 Graded Press, admin. by The Copyright Co., Nashville, TN

CD
Track
※32

Jesus Loves Me

C / G C / F / F C / C / G

Je - sus loves me! This I know, for the Bi - ble tells me so. Lit - tle ones to

C / F C C G C C / F /

Refrain

him be - long; they are weak, but he is strong. Yes, Je - sus loves me!

C / G / C / F / C/G / G7 C /

Yes, Je - sus loves me! Yes, Je - sus loves me! The Bi - ble tells me so.

WORDS: Anna B. Warner
MUSIC: William B. Bradbury

CD Track #31

Yes, Jesus loves me,

Yes, Jesus loves me,

Yes, Jesus loves me,

The Bible tells me so.

Love One Another

① C   F   G7   C

"Love one an - oth - er, love one an - oth - er,

② C   Dm   G7   C

love one an - oth - er," Je - sus said.

*May be sung as a two-part round.

WORDS: John 15:17
MUSIC: George Donigian
Music © 1991 Graded Press, admin. by The Copyright Co., Nashville, TN

Love — Cross hands at wrist and press over heart.

One another — Make a fist with both hands, thumbs out. Hold right fist with the thumb down. Hold the left fist with the thumb up. Circle the thumbs counter-clockwise around each other.

Jesus — Touch the middle finger of the right hand to the palm of the left hand. Reverse.

CD Track #33

Jesus Tells Stories

The Wise Man and the Foolish Man

Supplies: "The House on the Rock" (below and page 87), CD, CD player

Your children may already be familiar with the song "The House on the Rock" (below and page 87). Let them enjoy singing along and doing the motions as you play the song on the CD.

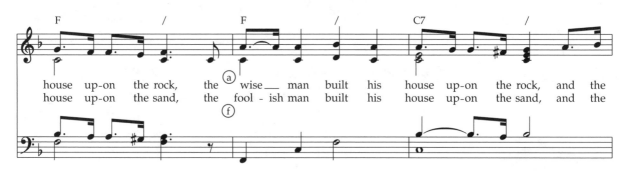

1. The ⓐ wise ___ man built his house up-on the rock, the ⓐ wise ___ man built his
2. The ⓕ fool-ish man built his house up-on the sand, the ⓕ fool-ish man built his

house up-on the rock, the ⓐ wise ___ man built his house up-on the rock, and the
house up-on the sand, the ⓕ fool-ish man built his house up-on the sand, and the

Actions:

ⓐ Pound on fist on top of the other in rhythm.
ⓑ Wiggle fingers while moving hands downward.
ⓒ Palms up, raise hands in rhythm.
ⓓ Fingertips form rooftop.
ⓔ Pound fists once.
ⓕ Pound fists into open palm in rhythm.
ⓖ Slap palms loudly.

CD Track #34

WORDS: Based on Matthew 7:24-27
MUSIC: Traditional; arr. by Nylea L. Butler-Moore

Arr. © 1993 Abingdon Press

Jesus Serves

Sing About Jesus' Love

Supplies: "If You Ask Me About Jesus" (below), CD, CD player

Play the song "If You Ask Me About Jesus" (below) on the CD. Encourage the children to move to the music.

If You Ask Me About Jesus

If you ask me a-bout Je-sus I will tell you a-bout love.
1. A-bout
2. A-bout

heal-ing, serv-ing, car-ing,
pray-ing, cel-e-brat-ing, he was sent by God a-bove.

WORDS and MUSIC: Denise A. Harris; transcription by David Bone
© 2000 Cokesbury

CD Track #35

Kind Hands

Supplies: "Jesus' Hands Were Kind Hands" (below), CD, CD player, handwashing supplies, finger-paint, large sheet of paper, marker

Let the children play with fingerpaint or make handprints. As they work, play "Jesus' Hands Were Kind Hands" (below) on the CD. Talk about the ways we use our hands. Help the children talk about kind things we can do with our hands. Ask the children about the kind things Jesus did with his hands. Make a handprint banner to share in worship, and sing the song for the congregation.

Jesus' Hands Were Kind Hands

1. Je - sus' hands were kind hands, do - ing good to all, heal - ing pain and
2. Take my hands, Lord Je - sus, let them work for you; make them strong and

sick - ness, bless - ing chil - dren small, wash - ing tir - ed feet, and
gen - tle, kind in all I do. Let me watch you, Je - sus,

sav - ing those who fall; Je - sus' hands were kind hands, do - ing good to all.
till I'm gen - tle too, till my hands are kind hands, quick to work for you.

WORDS: Margaret Cropper
MUSIC: Old French melody; harm. by Carlton R. Young
Words by permission of A. S. Hopkinson; harm. © 1989 The United Methodist Publishing House

CD Track #36

Jesus Calls Helpers

Play a Disciples Game

Supplies: "I Can Name Four Disciples" (page 91)

Say: The Bible tells us that Jesus asked people to be helpers. You can be a helper too. Let's play a game that will help us remember our Bible story.

Have the children stand in a circle. Play a game by singing "I Can Name Four Disciples" (page 91). Use the motions below as you sing the song, which is to the tune of "She'll Be Coming 'Round the Mountain."

I Can Name Four Disciples, yes I can *(Hold up four fingers)*
James and John, Peter and Andrew) *(Hold up one, then two, then three, then four fingers)*

Sing the song below to the refrain of "Bringing in the Sheaves." Call one child at a time to stand in the middle of the circle. For a large group, call several children at a time.

Jesus called us all. *(The children walk around in a circle.)*
Jesus called us all. *(The children walk around in a circle.)*
Clap our hands and stomp our feet. *(Clap your hands; stomp your feet.)*
Jesus called *(name of child)*. *(Have the child move to the middle of the circle.)*

This is a good game when you want the children to line up for an activity. Ask the children to sit on the floor and to line up as their name is called.

Jesus Fingerplay

You may wish to use the names of your children in the fingerplay below.

Jesus told other people about God's love.
  (Wiggle thumb.)
Andrew said, "I will tell about God's love."*(Wiggle first finger.)*
Run away, Andrew, and tell of God's love.
  (Move "Andrew" in a large circle in the air.)
Peter said, "I will tell about God's love." *(Wiggle second finger.)*
Run away, Peter, and tell of God's love.
  (Move "Peter" in a large circle in the air.)
Philip said, "I will tell about God's love." *(Wiggle third finger.)*
Run away, Philip, and tell of God's love.
  (Move "Philip" in a large circle in the air.)
Nathanael said, "I will tell about God's love."*(Wiggle fourth finger.)*
Run away, Nathanael, and tell of God's love.
  (Move "Nathanael" in a large circle in the air.)

I Can Name Four Disciples

I can name four dis-ci-ples, yes, I can. I can
name four dis-ci-ples, yes, I can. James and John, Pe-ter and An-drew, James and
John, Pe-ter and An-drew, I can name four dis-ci-ples, yes, I can.

WORDS: Melanie Hutto and Ann Thompson
MUSIC: Traditional
Words © 1991 Graded Press, admin. by The Copyright Co., Nashville, TN

Sing to the tune of "She'll Be Coming 'Round the Mountain"

Jesus Called

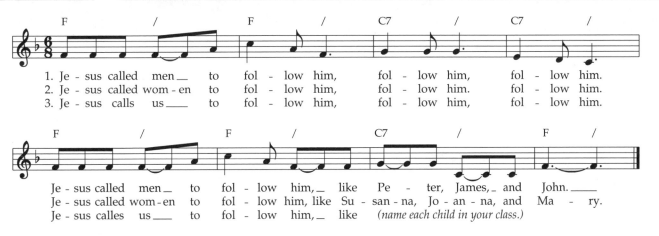

1. Je-sus called men__ to fol-low him, fol-low him, fol-low him.
2. Je-sus called wom-en to fol-low him, fol-low him. fol-low him.
3. Je-sus calls us__ to fol-low him, fol-low him, fol-low him.

Je-sus called men__ to fol-low him,__ like Pe-ter, James,__ and John.____
Je-sus called wom-en to fol-low him, like Su-san-na, Jo-an-na, and Ma-ry.
Je-sus calles us__ to fol-low him,__ like *(name each child in your class.)*

WORDS: Daphna Flegal
MUSIC: Traditional
Words © 1996 Cokesbury, admin. by The Copyright Co., Nashville, TN

Sing to the tune of "This Is the Way"

Jesus and the Children

The Children Come to See Jesus

Lead the children in the following fingerplay:

(*Hold up one finger.*)
One little child,
See him run,
Comes to see Jesus.
Oh, what fun!

(*Hold up two fingers.*)
Two little children,
See them walk,
Come to see Jesus
To laugh and talk.

(*Hold up three fingers.*)
Three little children,
See them hop,
Come to see Jesus,
And they won't stop.

(*Hold up four fingers.*)
Four little children,
See them prance,
Come to see Jesus.
Watch them dance!

(*Hold up five fingers.*)
Five little children,
See them skip,
Come to see Jesus.
What a happy trip!

Written by Sandy Svercek, Beth Parr, Nancy Coziahr, and Daphna Flegal.

Little Children

1. One lit-tle, two lit-tle, three lit-tle chil-dren, four lit-tle, five lit-tle, six lit-tle chil-dren,
2. Stop lit-tle chil-dren,_ don't go to Je-sus. Stop lit-tle chil-dren,_ don't go to Je-sus.
3. Come and_ sit with_ me, lit-tle chil-dren. Come and_ sit with_ me, lit-tle chil-dren.
4. One lit-tle, two lit-tle, three lit-tle chil-dren, four lit-tle, five lit-tle, six lit-tle chil-dren,

sev-en lit-tle, eight lit-tle, nine lit-tle chil-dren com-ing to see Je-sus.
Stop_ lit-tle chil-dren,_ don't go to Je-sus, he is much too bus-y.
Come_ and_ sit with_ me, lit-tle chil-dren, Je-sus loves the chil-dren.
sev-en lit-tle, eight lit-tle, nine lit-tle chil-dren hap-py to see Je-sus.

WORDS: Based on Mark 10:13-16
MUSIC: Traditional
Words © 1996 Cokesbury, admin. by The Copyright Co., Nashville, TN

Sing to the tune of "Ten Little Indians"

Jesus Loves the Little Children

Je - sus loves the lit - tle chil - dren, all the chil - dren of the world. Red, brown, yel - low, black, and white, they are pre - cious in his sight; Je - sus loves the lit - tle chil - dren of the world.

WORDS: Anonymous
MUSIC: George F. Root

CD Track ❋37

Bible Verse
Jesus said, "Let the children come to me."
Matthew 19:14a
Good News Translation

Called Christians

Supplies: "Have You Ever Seen a Christian?" (below), "I'm a Christian" (page 95)

Tell the children that followers of Jesus are called Christians. Teach the children the songs "Have You Ever Seen a Christian?" (below) and "I'm a Christian" (page 95).

1. Have you ev - er seen a Chris - tian, a Chris - tian, a Chris - tian? Have you
2. Have you ev - er seen a Chris - tian, a Chris - tian, a Chris - tian? Have you
3. Have you ev - er seen a Chris - tian, a Chris - tian, a Chris - tian? Have you
4. Have you ev - er seen a Chris - tian, a Chris - tian, a Chris - tian? Have you

ev - er seen a Chris - tian clap hands to praise God? Let's
ev - er seen a Chris - tian stand up to praise God? Let's
ev - er seen a Chris - tian stomp feet to praise God? Let's
ev - er seen a Chris - tian sit down to praise God? Let's

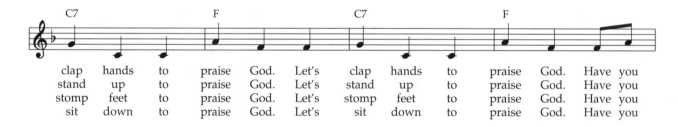

clap hands to praise God. Let's clap hands to praise God. Have you
stand up to praise God. Let's stand up to praise God. Have you
stomp feet to praise God. Let's stomp feet to praise God. Have you
sit down to praise God. Let's sit down to praise God. Have you

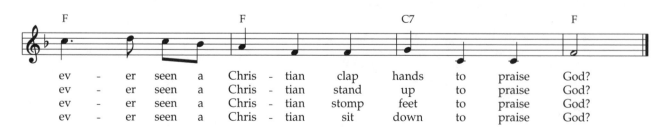

ev - er seen a Chris - tian clap hands to praise God?
ev - er seen a Chris - tian stand up to praise God?
ev - er seen a Chris - tian stomp feet to praise God?
ev - er seen a Chris - tian sit down to praise God?

WORDS: Daphna and Diana Flegal, from *More Bible Songs to Tunes You Know*
MUSIC: Traditional

Sing to the tune of "Did You Ever See a Lassie?"

I'm a Christian

Chorus

I'm a Chris-tian. Yes, I am a Chris-tian. I'm a Chris-tian. I

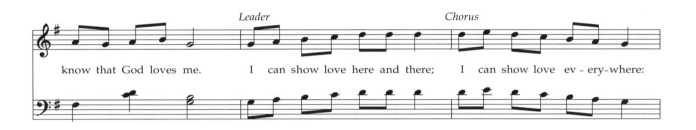

know that God loves me. **Leader** I can show love here and there; **Chorus** I can show love ev-ery-where:

Leader *
In my church, in my church. **Chorus** I'm a Chris-tian.
To my friends, to my friends.

Yes, I am a Chris-tian. I'm a Chris-tian. I know that God loves me.

*Continue to add lines as desired. Encourage the children to think of other places to add.

WORDS: Cynthia Gray, Linda Ray Miller, and Fran Porter
MUSIC: Traditional

Words © 2001 Cokesbury

Sing to the tune of "Alouette"

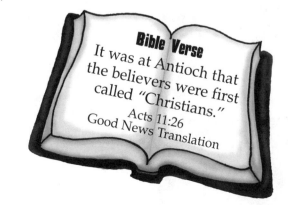

Bible Verse
It was at Antioch that the believers were first called "Christians."
Acts 11:26
Good News Translation

Paul

The Story of Paul

Supplies: Bible

Paul was mad, so the story goes,
Mad from his head down to his toes.
He wanted all followers of Jesus' way
Taken to prison for the rest of their days.
So off he went to another town,
Traveling the road up hill and down.

But before he'd traveled very far,
He saw a great light more bright than a star.
He heard Jesus speaking from the light,
And Paul made a change that very night.
Paul was sorry he'd treated people so bad.
Paul made a change from mad to glad.

Now because the light was so very bright,
Paul could not see for three days and nights.
Then Jesus spoke to another man
And asked Ananias to give Paul a hand.
Ananias was afraid at first,
For he had heard that Paul was the worst.

But Ananias went to Paul that day,
He taught Paul to follow Jesus' way.
Ananias helped Paul see again.
Paul and Ananias became good friends.
Paul began to teach and preach and pray.
Now Paul was a follower of Jesus' way.

(Based on Acts 9:1-22.)

Clap If You Love God

Supplies: "We Love" (page 98), CD, CD player

Tell the children that you are going to sing a song about love. Let them listen to the song "We Love" (page 98) on the CD. Then play the song again, leading them in clapping whenever it appears in the song.

Travel With Paul

Lead the children around your room using the following rhyme. Do the suggested motions as you move. End the activity in your story area. Always end with a very quiet movement in order to get the children ready for the story.

Let's walk to town with
(*Walk around the room.*)
Paul, Paul, Paul,
And tell about Jesus
To all, all, all.

We can go by camel.
(*Pretend to ride a camel.*)
We can go by horse.
(*Pretend to ride a horse.*)
We can even go by boat,
(*Pretend to row a boat.*)
Of course!

Let's hop to town with
(*Hop around the room.*)
Paul, Paul, Paul,
And tell about Jesus
To all, all, all.

We can go by camel.
(*Pretend to ride a camel.*)
We can go by horse.
(*Pretend to ride a horse.*)
We can even go by boat,
(*Pretend to row a boat.*)
Of course!

Let's march to town with
(*March around the room.*)
Paul, Paul, Paul,
And tell about Jesus
To all, all, all.

We can go by camel.
(*Pretend to ride a camel.*)
We can go by horse.
(*Pretend to ride a horse.*)
We can even go by boat,
(*Pretend to row a boat.*)
Of course!

Let's tiptoe to town with
(*Tiptoe around the room.*)
Paul, Paul, Paul,
And tell about Jesus
To all, all, all.

We can go by camel.
(*Pretend to ride a camel.*)
We can go by horse.
(*Pretend to ride a horse.*)
We can even go by boat,
(*Pretend to row a boat.*)
Of course!

We Love

WORDS: 1 John 4:19
MUSIC: Ann F. Price; arr. by Nylea L. Butler-Moore

CD Track #38

The Early Church

Rhythm Round

Have the children sit in a circle on the floor. Begin patting your thighs and clapping your hands in a rhythmic pattern: pat, pat, clap, clap, pat, pat, clap. Encourage the children to do the rhythm pattern with you. (Young children may not keep the rhythm going. Have a good time anyway.) When everyone is comfortable with the pattern, explain that you are going to ask each child a question. Each child will answer, "Yes, I do!" Have the children practice the response (see below). Repeat the poem for each child.

Tell me, (*child's name*),
　(*Pat, pat, clap the number of syllables
　　in the child's name.*)
Tell me true, (*Pat, pat, clap.*)

Do you know that (*Pat, pat, clap, clap.*)
God loves you? (*Pat, pat, clap.*)
Have the child respond:
Yes, I do! (*Pat, pat, clap.*)

Following Jesus

Supplies: "Paul Became a Follower" (below)

Teach the children the song "Paul Became a Follower" (below). The song is sung to the tune of "Do You Know the Muffin Man?"

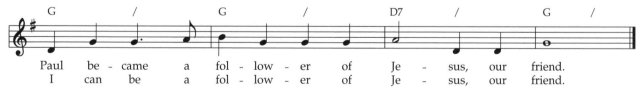

WORDS: Based on Acts 9:1-19
MUSIC: Traditional
Words © 1996 Cokesbury, admin. by The Copyright Co., Nashville, TN

Sing to the tune of "Do You Know the Muffin Man?"

Move to "Paul and Lydia"

Supplies: "Paul and Lydia" (below); purple ribbons, streamers, or scarfs

Have the children join you in an open area of the room. Give the children purple ribbons, streamers, or scarfs. Remind the children that Lydia sold purple cloth.

Sing "Paul and Lydia" (below). Let the children move their streamers to the music. Remind the children that Lydia and everyone at her house became Christians. The song is sung to the tune of "Down By the Riverside."

Bible Verse
Let all that you do be done in love.
1 Corinthians 16:14

Paul and Lydia

1. I know that Paul___ met Lyd-i-a down by the riv-er-side,
2. I know that Paul___ told Lyd-i-a down by the riv-er-side,
3. I know the Paul bap-tized Lyd-i-a down by the riv-er-side,

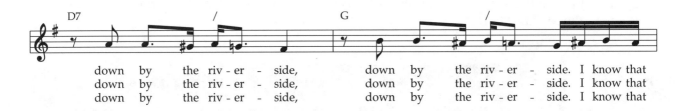

down by the riv-er-side, down by the riv-er-side. I know that
down by the riv-er-side, down by the riv-er-side. I know that
down by the riv-er-side, down by the riv-er-side. I know that

Paul___ met Lyd-i-a down by the riv-er-side,___
Paul___ told Lyd-i-a down by the riv-er-side,___
Paul bap-tized Lyd-i-a down by the riv-er-side, and

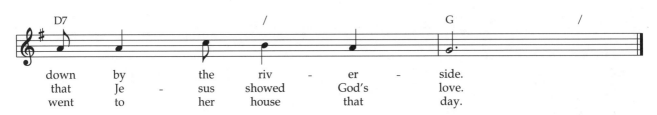

down by the riv-er-side.
that Je-sus showed God's love.
went to her house that day.

WORDS: Doris Willis
MUSIC: Traditional

Words © 1986 Graded Press, admin. by The Copyright Co., Nashville, TN

Sing to the tune of "Down by the Riverside"

100

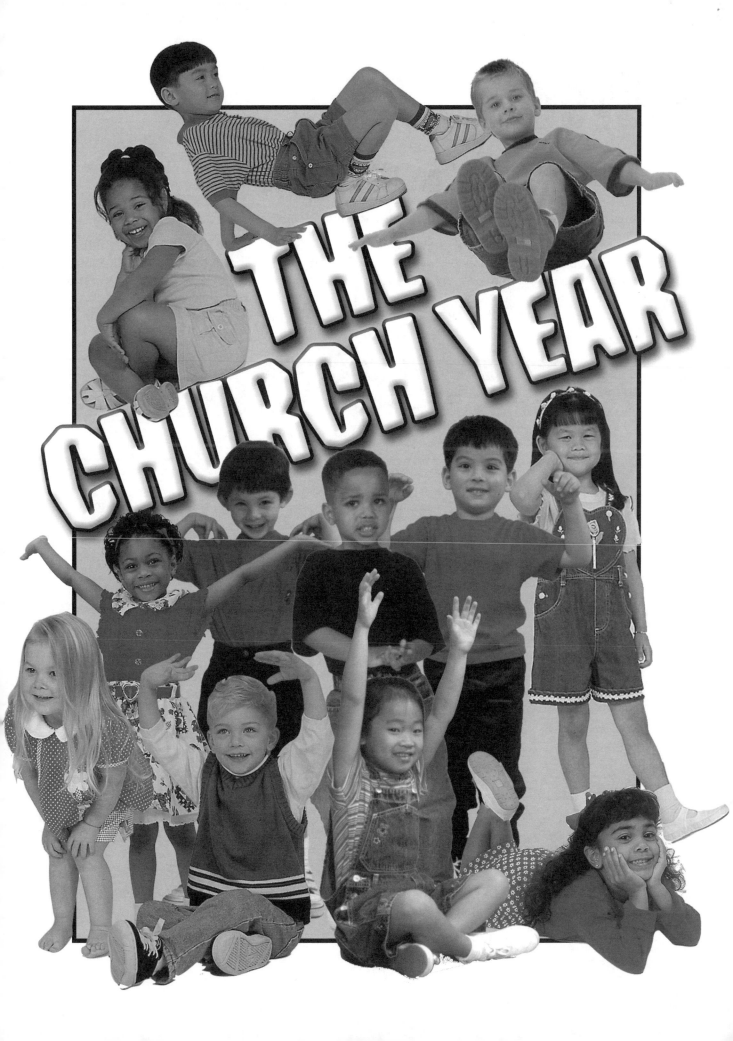

Advent

Getting Ready for Christmas

Supplies: "Let's Get Ready" (below), Advent wreath, matches

Sing the song "Let's Get Ready" (below) as an echo song. Sing each line, then have the children repeat the line with you. As you do this each week, the children will become so familiar with the song that they may be able to repeat their lines without you. Sing the first verse of this song on the first Sunday of Advent as you light your Advent wreath. Sing the second verse on the second Sunday of Advent, the third verse on the third Sunday, and so on.

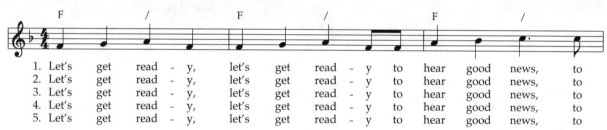

1. Let's get read - y, let's get read - y to hear good news, to
2. Let's get read - y, let's get read - y to hear good news, to
3. Let's get read - y, let's get read - y to hear good news, to
4. Let's get read - y, let's get read - y to hear good news, to
5. Let's get read - y, let's get read - y to hear good news, to

hear good news. _____ An an - gel came to Mar - y, an
hear good news. _____ Go with us to Beth - le - hem, _____
hear good news. _____ Wel - come, ba - by Je - sus, _____
hear good news. _____ The shep - herds saw the ba - by, the
hear good news. _____ Wise men saw the bright ___ star, _____

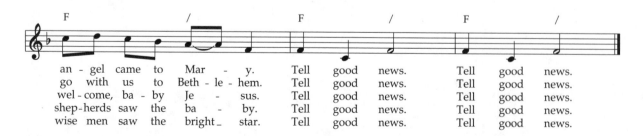

an - gel came to Mar - y. Tell good news. Tell good news.
go with us to Beth - le - hem. Tell good news. Tell good news.
wel - come, ba - by Je - sus. Tell good news. Tell good news.
shep - herds saw the ba - by. Tell good news. Tell good news.
wise men saw the bright ___ star. Tell good news. Tell good news.

WORDS: Fran Porter, Cynthia Gray, Linda Ray Miller
MUSIC: Traditional
Words © 2000 Cokesbury

Sing to the tune of "Are You Sleeping?"

Make Nonflammable Candles

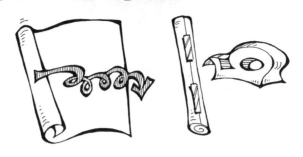

Supplies: tape, tissue paper, purple or blue construction paper

1. Roll a piece of purple or blue construction paper into a long cylinder.

2. Tape it closed to make it fit your candleholder.

3. Take a 3-inch square of tissue paper and fold it in half and in half again.

4. Push the bottom corner gently into the top of the "candle" to make a "lit" candle.

5. Each week, add another tissue "flame" to your Advent wreath.

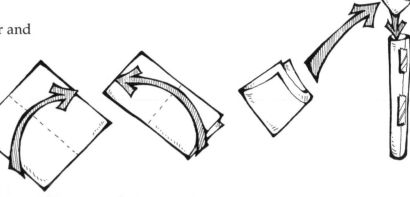

Light the Advent Candles

Light the ad-vent can-dles, see them burn-ing bright. Hope, love, joy, and peace tell the sto-ry Christ-mas night.

WORDS: Charles L. Terrell, Jr.
MUSIC: Traditional, adapt. by Charles L. Terrell, Jr. and Patricia A. Terrell

CD Track #39

Palm Sunday

Wave Palm Branches

Supplies: "Hosanna" (below), CD, CD player, palm branches (real or artificial)

Use the refrain "Hosanna" (below) as a processional, perhaps in your congregation's worship. Traditionally, palm branches have been waved by church members while the choir and the pastor (representing Jesus and the disciples) process down the aisle.

Give each of the children palm branches (real or artificial) and show them how to wave them high over their heads. Show them that a gentle waving back and forth is all that is needed for a dramatic effect. This will also cut down on accidentally hitting someone's face with a palm branch. Play "Hosanna" on the CD while the children wave their branches.

WORDS and MUSIC: Joyce Whitehead Elliott

Move to the Bible Story

Say: Let's pretend we are donkeys carrying Jesus into the city. Watch me and do what I do.

Walk, little donkeys! All around.
(*Pat your legs in an alternating pattern.*)
Now stand very still; don't make a sound!
(*Hold your hands still.*)
Hee haw. Hee haw. Do you see those men?
(*Hold your hands above your eyes.*)
They have come to get you for Jesus, their friend.
(*Hold your hands over your heart.*)
Walk little donkeys, over the hill;
(*Pat your legs in an alternating pattern.*)
Look, there's Jesus, so now stand still.
(*Hold your hands still.*)
You carry Jesus right down the street.
(*Pat your legs in an alternating pattern.*)
You see the palm branches laid at your feet.
(*Sweep the floor with your hand.*)
You hear the crowd shouting, "Blessed is the one!"
(*Cup your hand over your ear.*)
You're very happy as you walk in the sun.
(*Pat your legs in an alternating pattern.*)

Bible Verse
Blessed is the one who comes in the name of the Lord!
Mark 11:9

Hosanna!

1. He'll be rid-ing on a don-key when he comes. He'll be
2. Oh, we'll all ___ shout, "Ho-san-na" when he comes. Oh, we'll

rid-ing on a don-key when he comes. He'll be rid-ing on a don-key, he'll be
all ___ shout, "Ho-san-na" when he comes. Oh, we'll all ___ shout, "Ho-san-na." Oh, we'll

rid-ing on a don-key, he'll be rid-ing on a don-key when he comes.
all ___ shout, "Ho-san-na!" Oh, we'll all ___ shout, "Ho-san-na!" when he comes.

WORDS: Daphna Flegal
MUSIC: Traditional
Words © 1997 Abingdon Press, admin. by The Copyright Co., Nashville, TN

Sing to the tune of "She'll Be Coming 'Round the Mountain"

The Last Supper

Say the Bible Verse

Supplies: "Jesus Shared a Special Meal" (below),"A Special Meal" (page 107), CD, CD player plastic or paper cup (optional: unbreakable communion chalice)

Show the children a plastic or paper cup. If you have access to an unbreakable communion chalice, this would be ideal.

Say: Jesus shared a special meal with his friends. At the meal Jesus thanked God for the bread and juice and shared them with his friends. Jesus said, "Do this in memory of me" (Luke 22:19, Good News Translation).

Have the children sit in a circle. Pass the cup to the child next to you while singing the first verse of "Jesus Shared a Special Meal" (below). Have the children pass the cup as you sing. At the end of the verse, ask the child holding the cup to say the Bible verse, "Do this in memory of me." Sing the second verse while passing the cup. At the end of the verse, ask another child to say the verse. Continue passing and singing until all the children have said the Bible verse. You may choose to do this activity while playing "A Special Meal" (page 107) and pushing "pause" when you want a child to say the Bible verse.

Jesus Shared a Special Meal

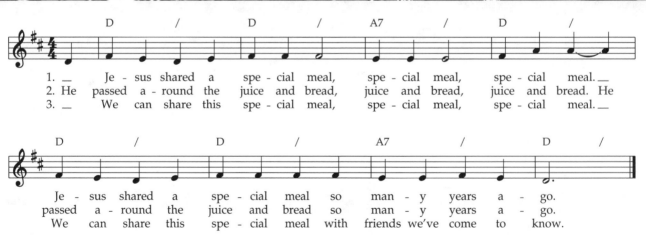

1. _ Je - sus shared a spe - cial meal, spe - cial meal, spe - cial meal. _
2. He passed a - round the juice and bread, juice and bread, juice and bread. He
3. _ We can share this spe - cial meal, spe - cial meal, spe - cial meal. _

Je - sus shared a spe - cial meal so man - y years a - go.
passed a - round the juice and bread so man - y years a - go.
We can share this spe - cial meal with friends we've come to know.

WORDS: Tim Edmonds
MUSIC: Traditional
Words © 1996 Cokesbury, admin. by The Copyright Co., Nashville, TN

Sing to the tune of "Mary Had a Little Lamb"

A Special Meal

Light and detached

1. Je - sus shared a spe - cial meal __
2. We re - mem - ber how he shared this

man - y years a - go.
meal of long a - go

He passed the bread and
by eat - ing bread and

last time

juice a-round to friends he'd come to know.
drink - ing juice with friends we've come to know.

WORDS and MUSIC: Timothy Edmonds

© 1990 Graded Press, admin. by The Copyright Co., Nashville, TN

Bible Verse
Do this in memory of me.
Luke 22:19,
Good News Translation

CD Track #41

Easter

Five Little Children

Bible Verse
The Lord has risen indeed!
Luke 24:34

Teach your children the following fingerplay:

Five little children came to church on Easter day.
(*Wiggle all five fingers.*)
The first child said, "Let's all shout, 'Hurray!'"
(*Hold up one finger.*)
The second child said, "God brings new life in spring."
(*Hold up two fingers.*)
The third child said, "Hear the church bells ring."
(*Hold up three fingers.*)
The fourth child said, "Let's all sing for joy."
(*Hold up four fingers.*)
The fifth child said, "God loves every girl and boy."
(*Hold up five fingers.*)
Five little children came to church to learn and play.
They all knew Easter was a very happy day.
(*Wiggle all five fingers.*)

Going to the Tomb

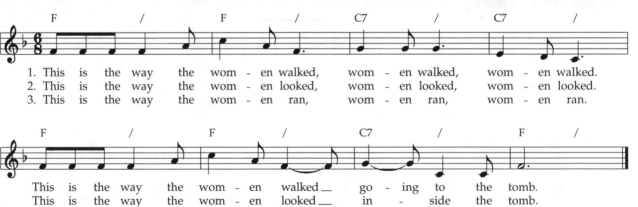

1. This is the way the wom-en walked, wom-en walked, wom-en walked.
2. This is the way the wom-en looked, wom-en looked, wom-en looked.
3. This is the way the wom-en ran, wom-en ran, wom-en ran.

This is the way the wom-en walked___ go-ing to the tomb.
This is the way the wom-en looked___ in-side the tomb.
This is the way the wom-en ran to tell_____ the good news.

WORDS: Linda Ray Miller
MUSIC: Traditional

Sing to the tune of "This Is the Way"

Jesus Lives

Teach your children the words *Jesus lives* in American Sign Language. Say the following poem for your children. Have the children sign the last line.

Easter is a special day
To dance and sing
And shout and pray.
So listen as our thanks we give,
For Jesus lives; Jesus lives!

Jesus — Touch the middle finger of the right hand to the left palm. Reverse.

Lives — Form an "L" with each hand as shown. Bring your hands up from your waist to in front of your chest.

Easter Day

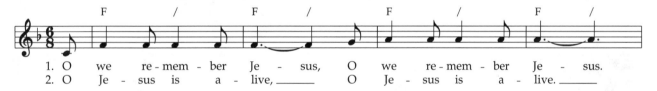

1. O we re-mem-ber Je - sus, O we re-mem-ber Je - sus.
2. O Je - sus is a - live, _____ O Je - sus is a - live. _____

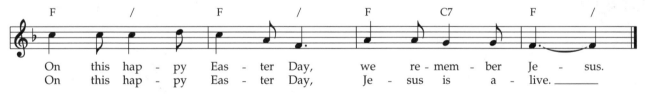

On this hap - py Eas - ter Day, we re-mem - ber Je - sus.
On this hap - py Eas - ter Day, Je - sus is a - live. _____

WORDS: Daphna Flegal
MUSIC: Traditional
Words © 1997 Abingdon Press, admin. by The Copyright Co., Nashville, TN

Sing to the tune of "The Farmer in the Dell"

Pentecost

Wave Streamers and Dance

Supplies: "Pentecost Day" (below); orange, red, and yellow crepe paper, tape

Make streamers of orange, red, and yellow crepe paper. Tape a ten-inch strip of each color together at one end. Give each child a set of two streamers. Encourage the children to dance with the streamers as you listen to "Pentecost Day" (below).

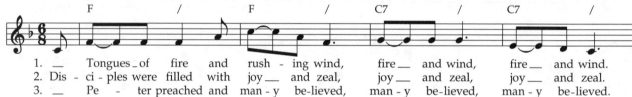

1. __ Tongues __ of fire and rush - ing wind, fire __ and wind, fire __ and wind.
2. Dis - ci - ples were filled with joy __ and zeal, joy __ and zeal, joy __ and zeal.
3. __ Pe - ter preached and man - y be-lieved, man - y be-lieved, man - y be-lieved.

Signs of the Ho - ly Spir - it with - in on that Pen - te - cost Day. _____
Tell - ing good news __ that Je - sus lives on that Pen - te - cost Day. _____
Thou-sands were bap-tized, the church __ was born on that Pen - te - cost Day. _____

WORDS: Ruth Wiertzema and Bob Landis
MUSIC: Traditional

Words © 1995 Cokesbury, admin. by The Copyright Co., Nashville, TN

Sing to the tune of "This Is the Way"

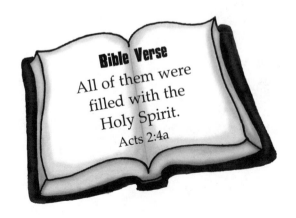

Bible Verse
All of them were filled with the Holy Spirit.
Acts 2:4a

Index by Title of Song or Fingerplay

Items in bold are songs.

CD Index

1. The B-I-B-L-E
2. God Plans for Every Growing Thing
3. Creation Dance
4. Noah
5. A Little Camel Music
6. Abraham's Family
7. Sarah Had a Baby Boy
8. I Will Be With You
9. Tiny Baby in the Water
10. Little Baby Moses
11. Holy Moses Stomp
12. Moses Parts the Red Sea
13. Sing and Celebrate
14. Little Samuel Grew
15. A Friend Loves at All Times
16. Clap Your Hands
17. Wiggle Praise
18. Praise God
19. Lion Music
20. Gonna Build a Wall
21. Clippity Clop
22. Donkey Music
23. The Angel Band
24. Away in a Manger
25. Little Jesus
26. The Friendly Beasts
27. Star Music
28. Amen
29. Jesus Learned About God
30. Drip, Drop, Splish, Splash
31. Jesus Loves Me
32. If I Had a Drum
33. Love One Another
34. The House on the Rock
35. If You Ask Me About Jesus
36. Jesus' Hands Were Kind Hands
37. Jesus Loves the Little Children
38. We Love
39. Light the Advent Candles
40. Hosanna
41. A Special Meal

CD Credits